FOR ORGANS, PIANOS & ELECTRONIC KEYBOARDS

E-Z PLAY TODAY
288

S0-BEB-076

Sing-A-Long
Christmas Favorites

ISBN 0-7935-4885-3

HAL•LEONARD™
CORPORATION
7777 W. BLUEMOUND RD. P.O. BOX 13819 MILWAUKEE, WI 53213

FOR ORGANS, PIANOS & ELECTRONIC KEYBOARDS

E-Z PLAY TODAY

288

Sing-A-Long Christmas Favorites

Blue Christmas

Registration 3
Rhythm: Fox Trot or Swing

Words and Music by Billy Hayes
and Jay Johnson

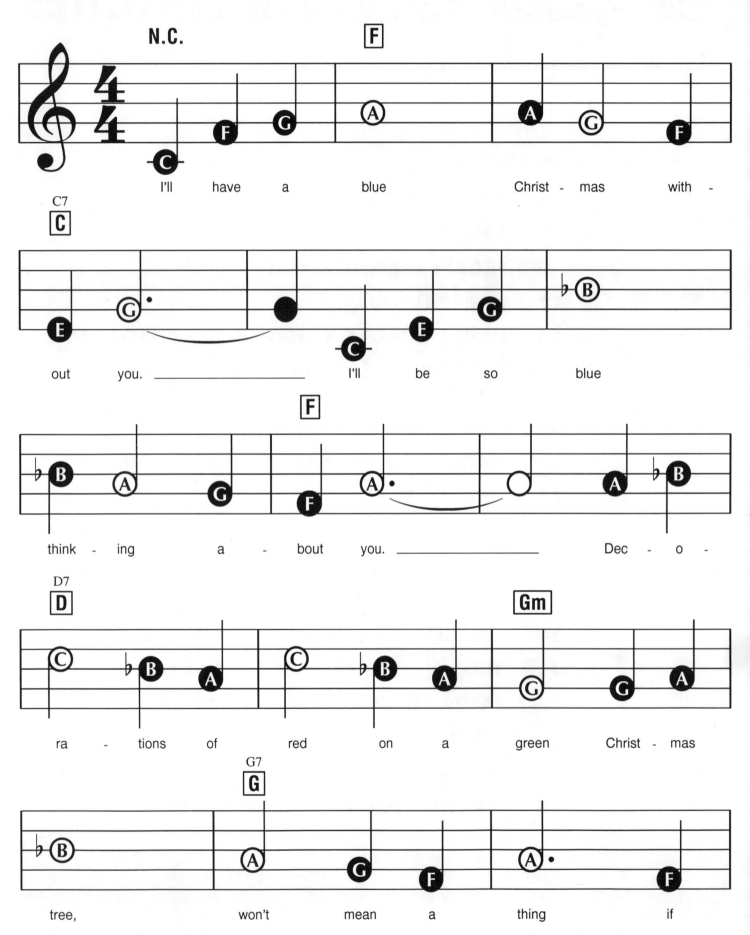

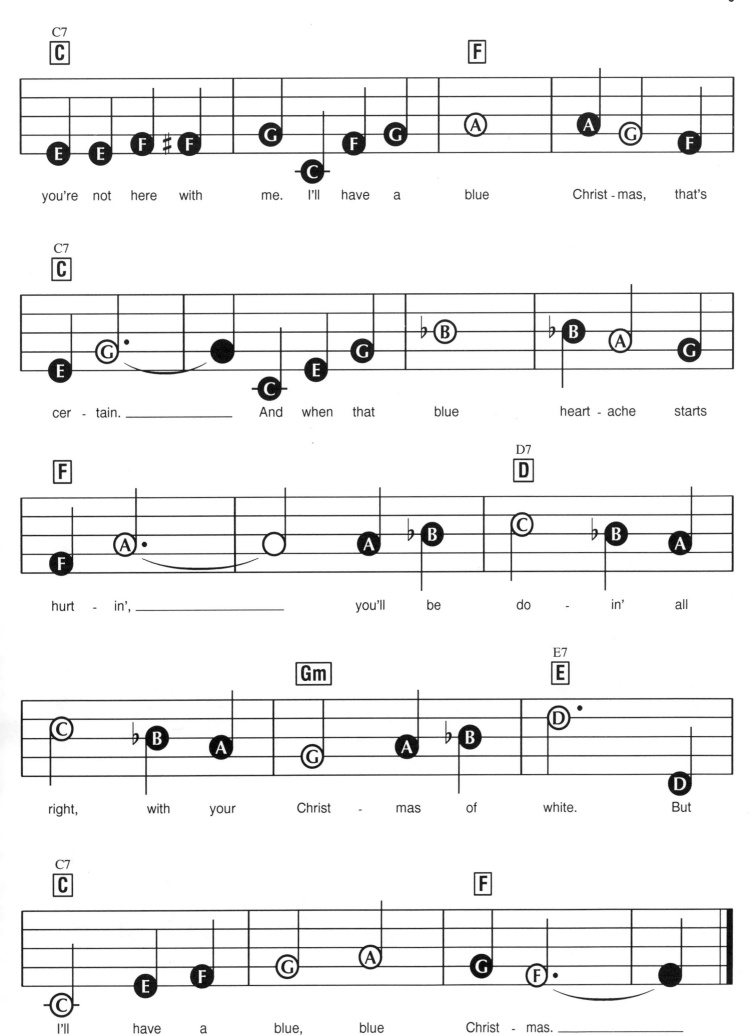

Deck The Hall

Registration 5

Traditional

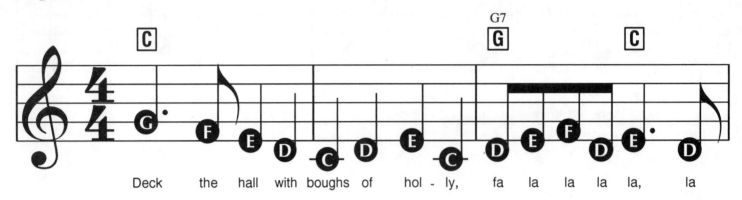

Deck the hall with boughs of hol - ly, fa la la la la, la

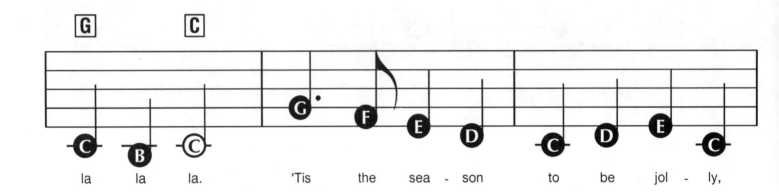

la la la. 'Tis the sea - son to be jol - ly,

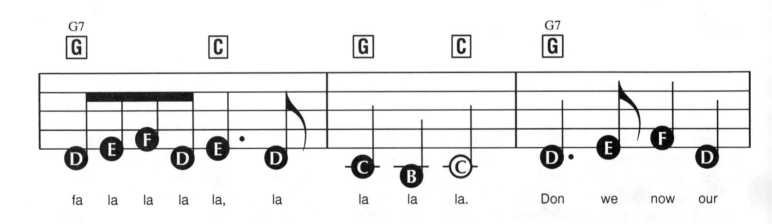

fa la la la la, la la la la. Don we now our

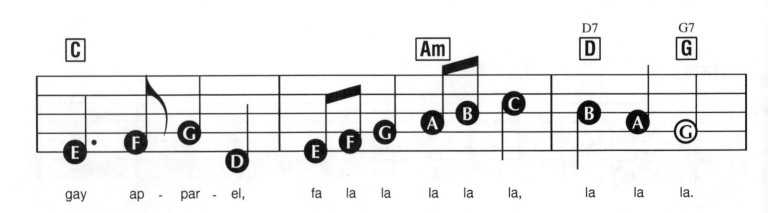

gay ap - par - el, fa la la la la la, la la la.

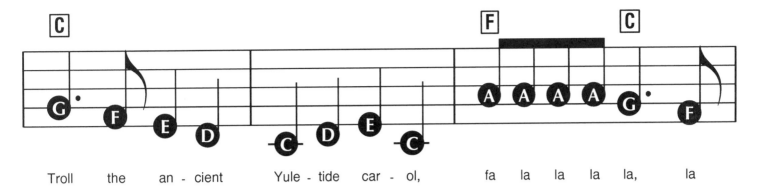

Troll the an-cient Yule-tide car-ol, fa la la la la, la

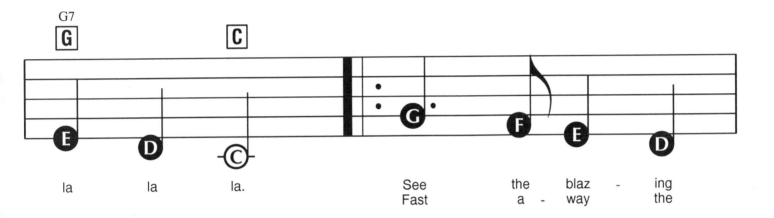

la la la. See the blaz - ing
Fast a - way the

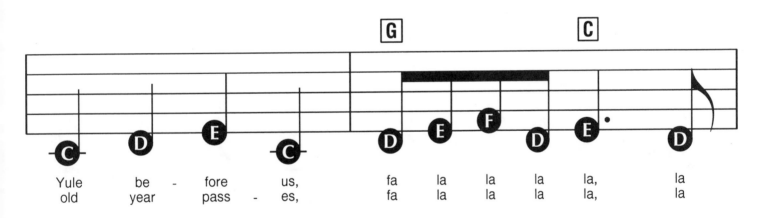

Yule be - fore us, fa la la la la, la la
old year pass - es, fa la la la la, la

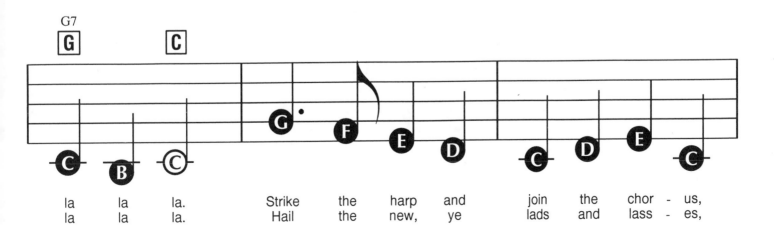

la la la. Strike the harp and join the chor - us,
la la la. Hail the new, ye lads and lass - es,

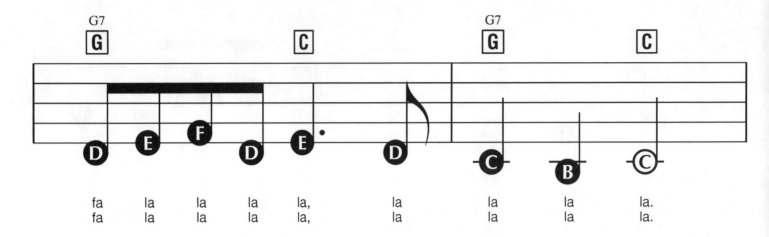

fa la la la la, la la la la.
fa la la la la, la la la la.

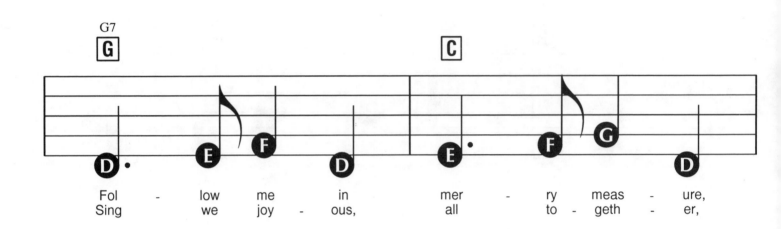

Fol - low me in mer - ry meas - ure,
Sing we joy - ous, all to - geth - er,

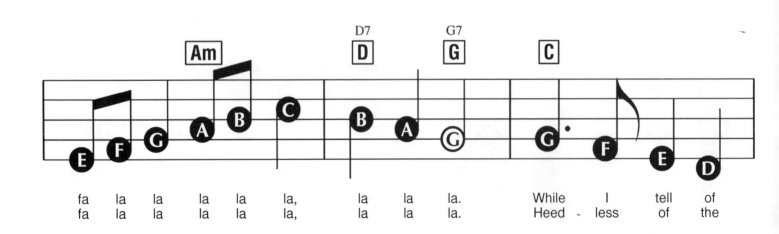

fa la la la la la, la la la. While I tell of
fa la la la la la, la la la. Heed - less of the

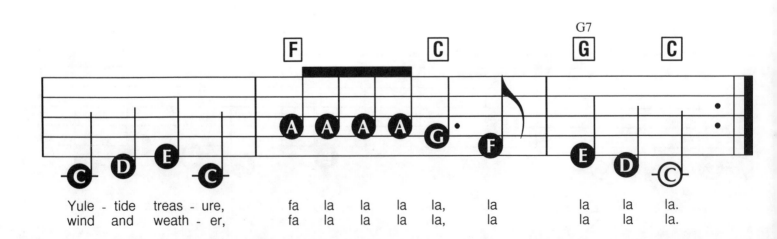

Yule - tide treas - ure, fa la la la la, la la la la.
wind and weath - er, fa la la la la, la la la la.

Frosty The Snow Man

Registration 2
Rhythm: Fox Trot or Swing

Words and Music by Steve Nelson
and Jack Rollins

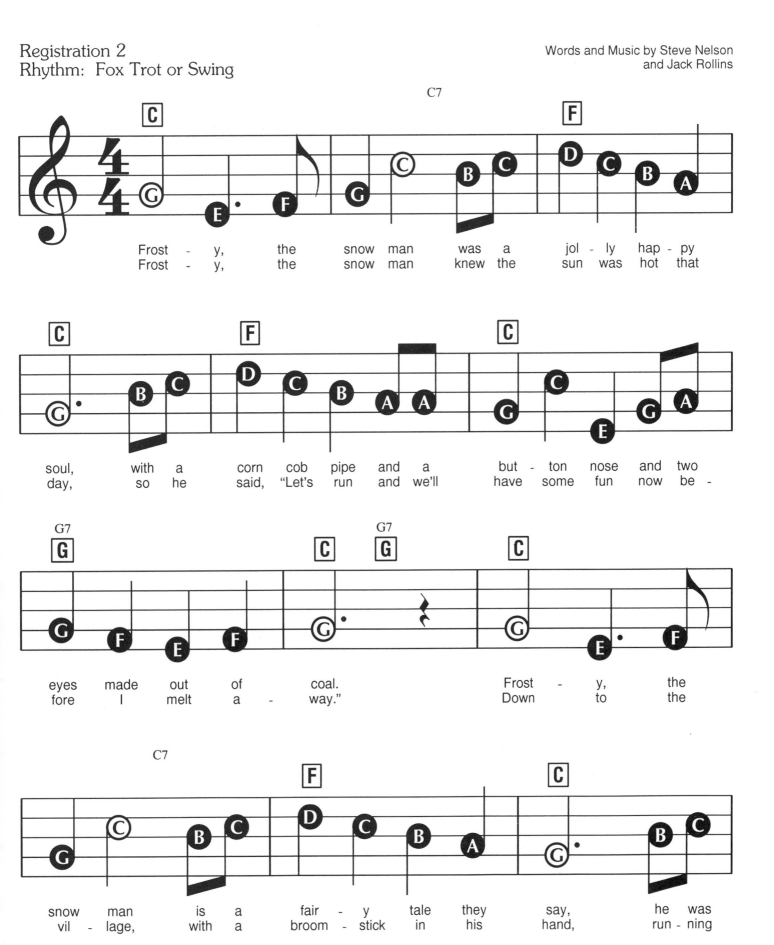

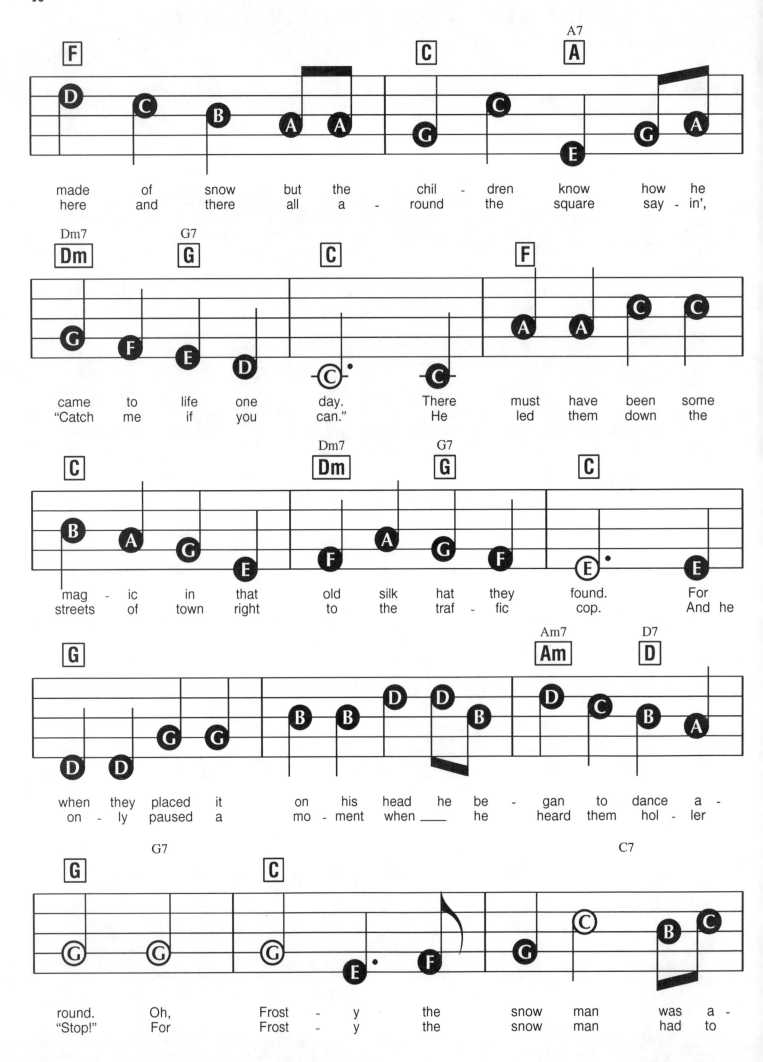

live as he could be, and the chil - dren say he could
hur - ry on his way, but he waved good - bye say - in',

laugh and play, just the same as you and
"Don't you cry, I'll be back a - gain some

me. Thump - et - y thump thump, thump - et - y thump thump
day."

look at Frost - y go. Thump - et - y thump thump,

thump - et - y thump thump o - ver the hills of snow.

Happy Holiday

Registration 4
Rhythm: Fox Trot or Ballad

Words and Music by
Irving Berlin

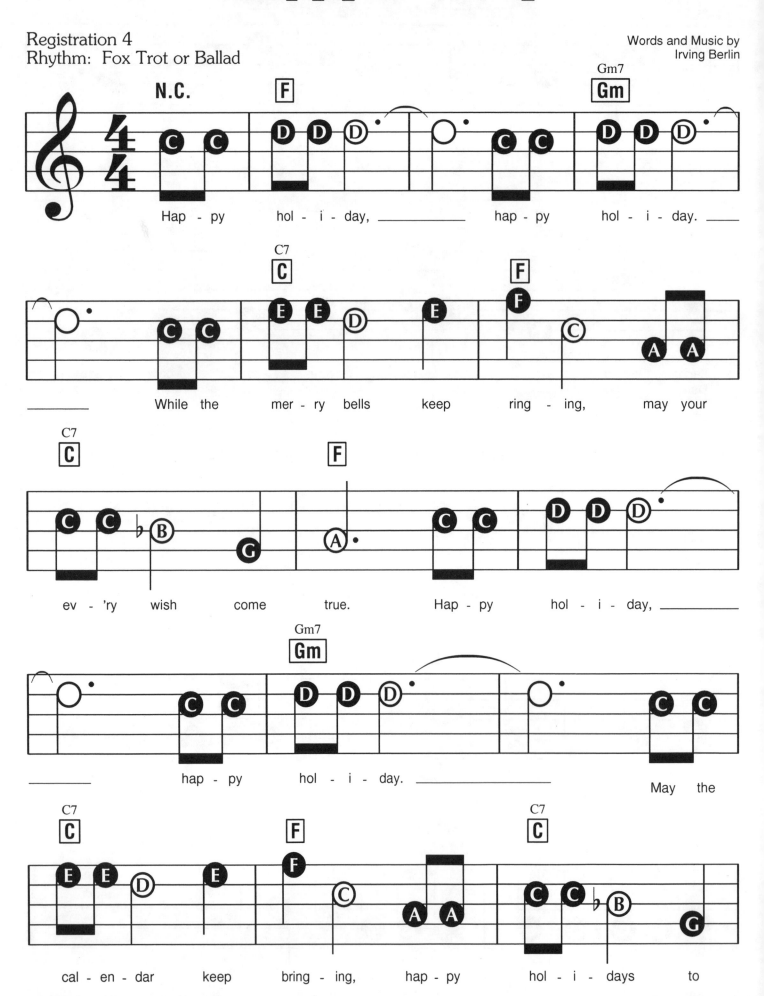

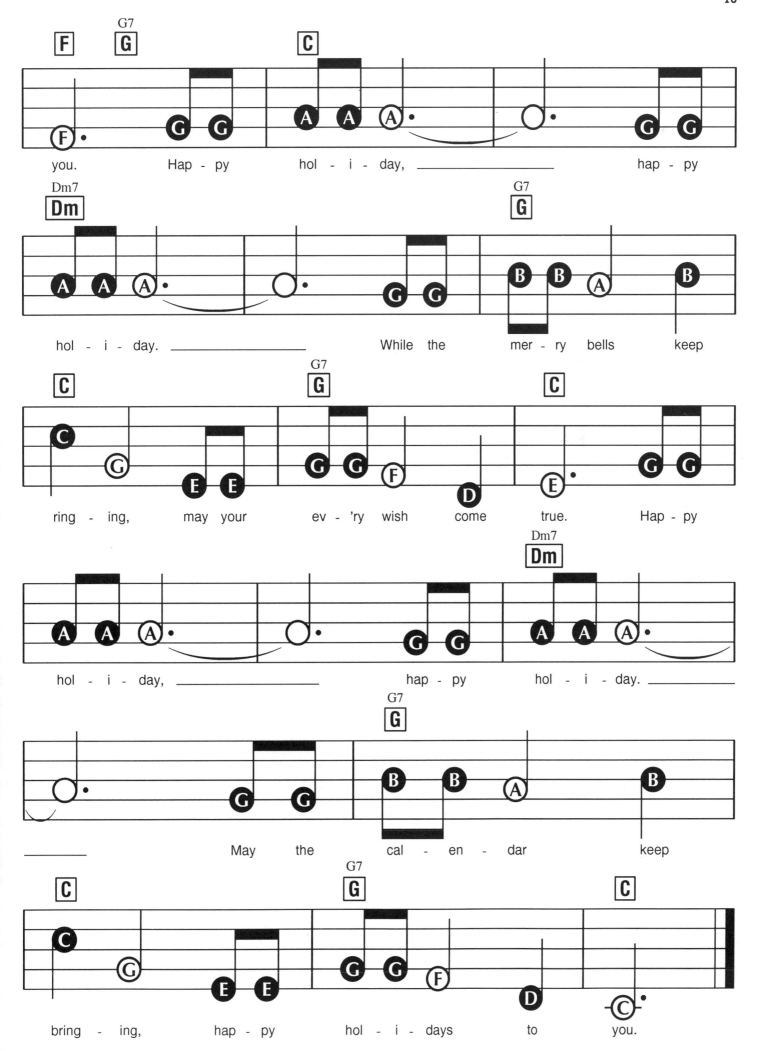

Have Yourself A Merry Little Christmas

Registration 7
Rhythm: Fox Trot or Swing

Words and Music by Ralph Blane
and Hugh Martin

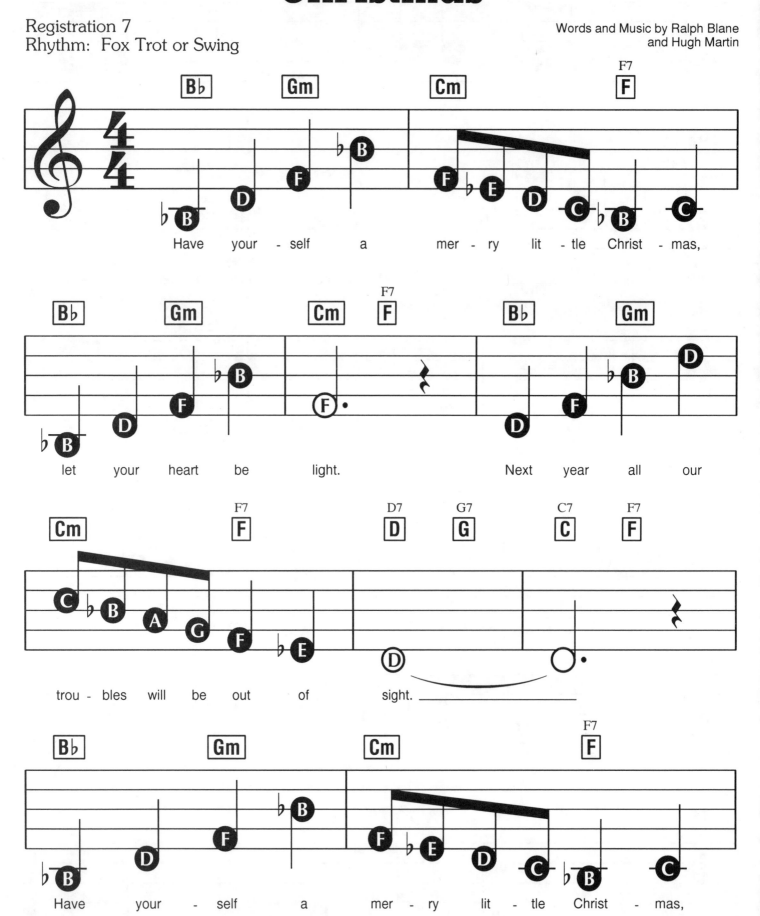

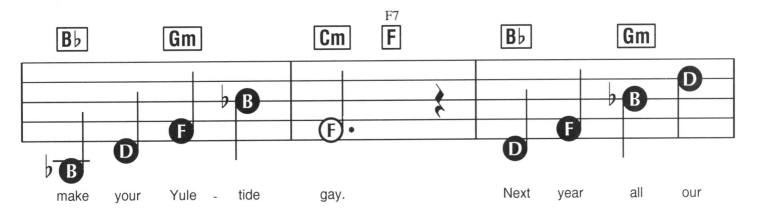

make your Yule - tide gay.   Next year all our

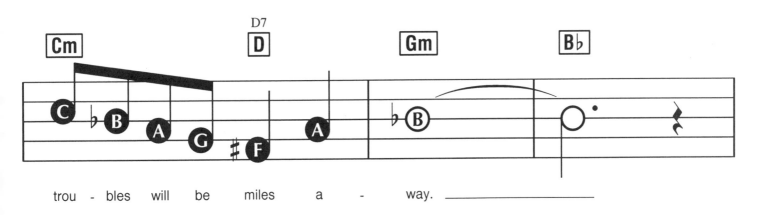

trou - bles will be miles a - way. _____

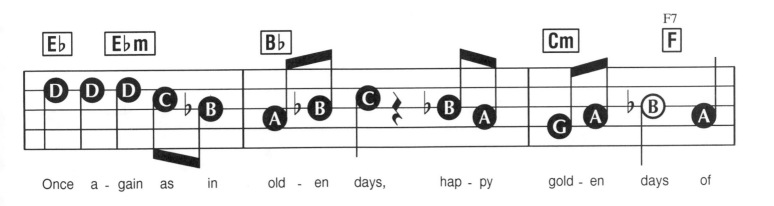

Once a - gain as in old - en days, hap - py gold - en days of

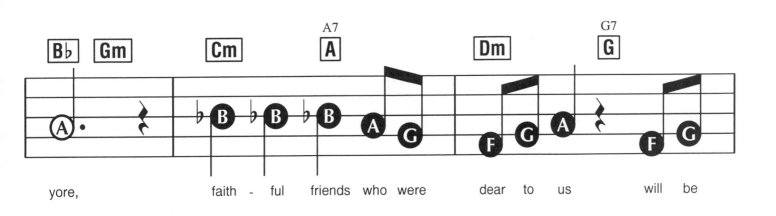

yore,   faith - ful friends who were dear to us will be

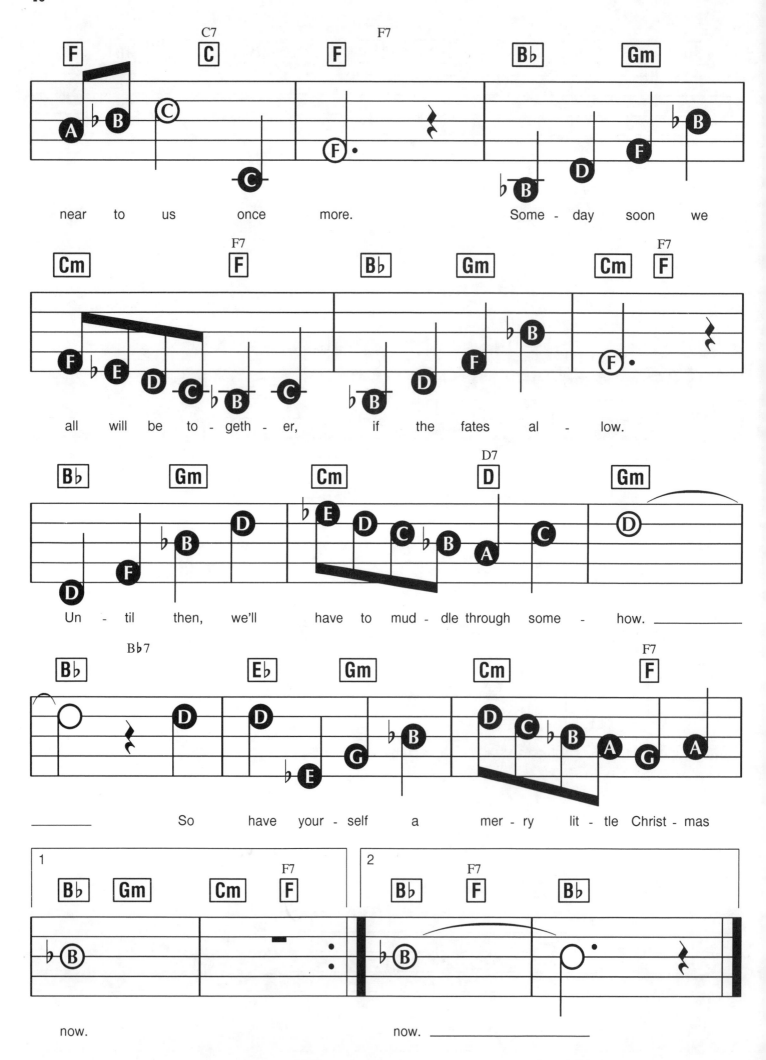

Here Comes Santa Claus
(Right Down Santa Claus Lane)

Registration 4
Rhythm: Swing

Words and Music by Gene Autry
and Oakley Haldeman

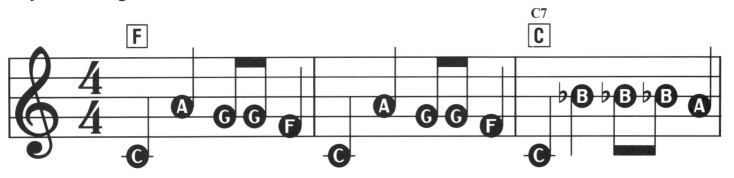

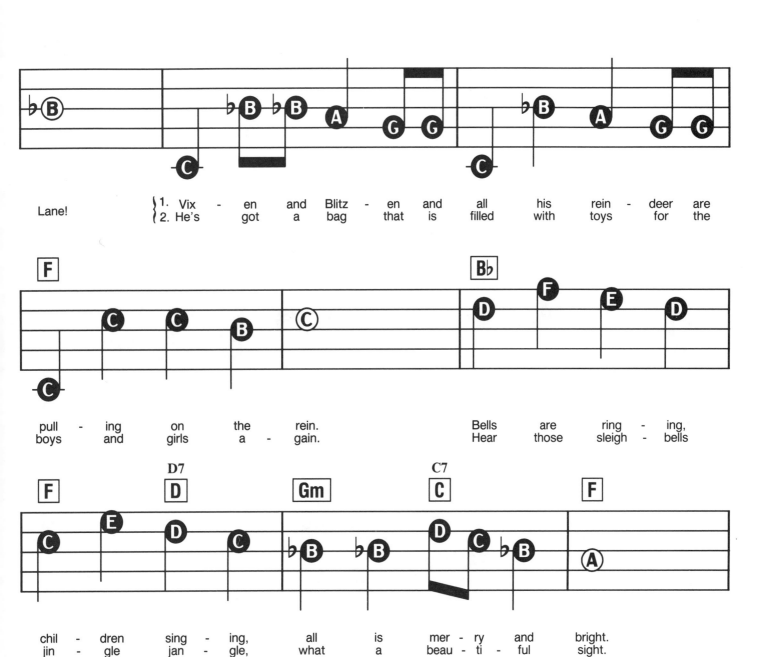

Here comes San - ta Claus! Here comes San - ta Claus! Right down San - ta Claus

Lane!
1. Vix - en and Blitz - en and all his rein - deer are
2. He's got a bag that is all filled with toys for the

pull - ing on the rein. Bells are ring - ing,
boys and girls a - gain. Hear those sleigh - bells

chil - dren sing - ing, all is mer - ry and bright.
jin - gle jan - gle, what a beau - ti - ful sight.

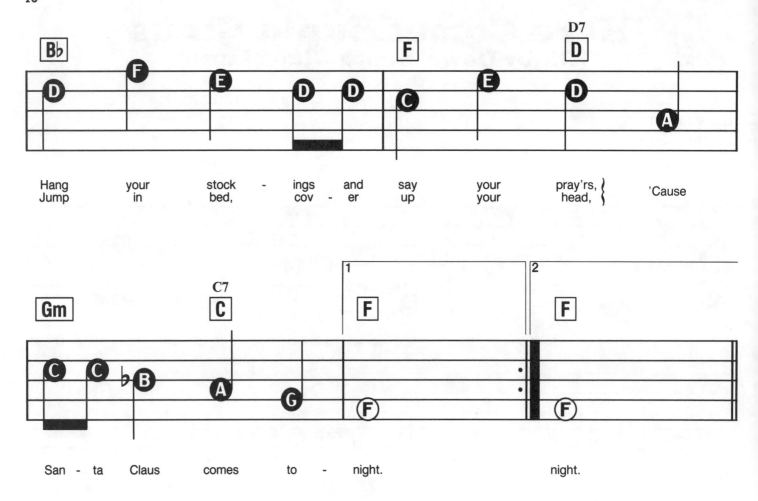

Hang your stock - ings and say your pray'rs, } 'Cause
Jump in bed, cov - er up your head, }

San - ta Claus comes to - night. night.

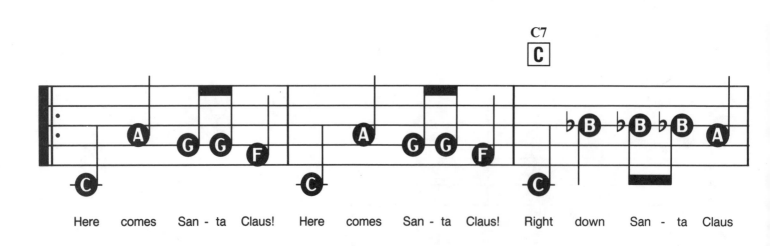

Here comes San - ta Claus! Here comes San - ta Claus! Right down San - ta Claus

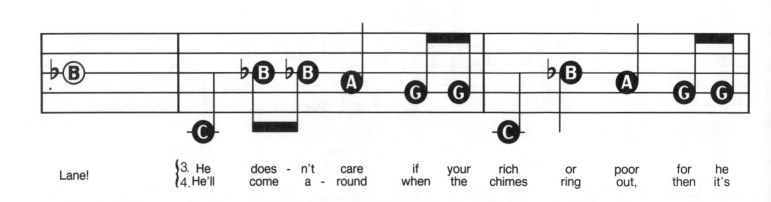

Lane!
{ 3. He does - n't care if your rich or poor, for he
{ 4. He'll come a - round when the chimes ring out, then it's

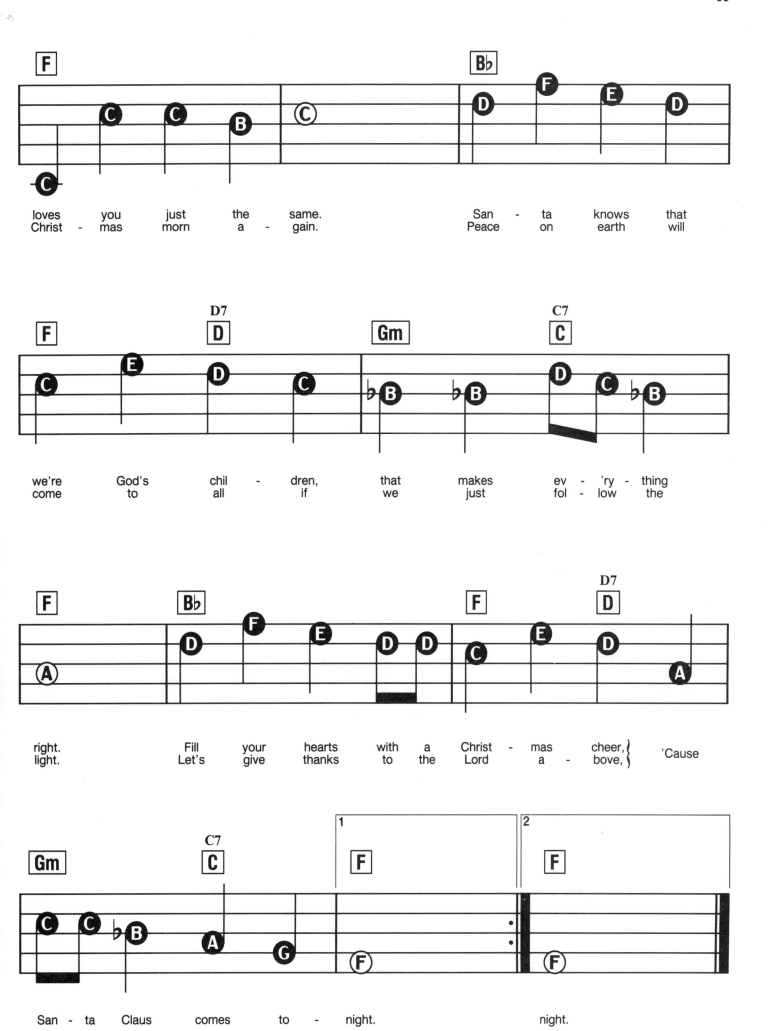

A Holly Jolly Christmas

Registration 9
Rhythm: Swing

Music and Lyrics by
Johnny Marks

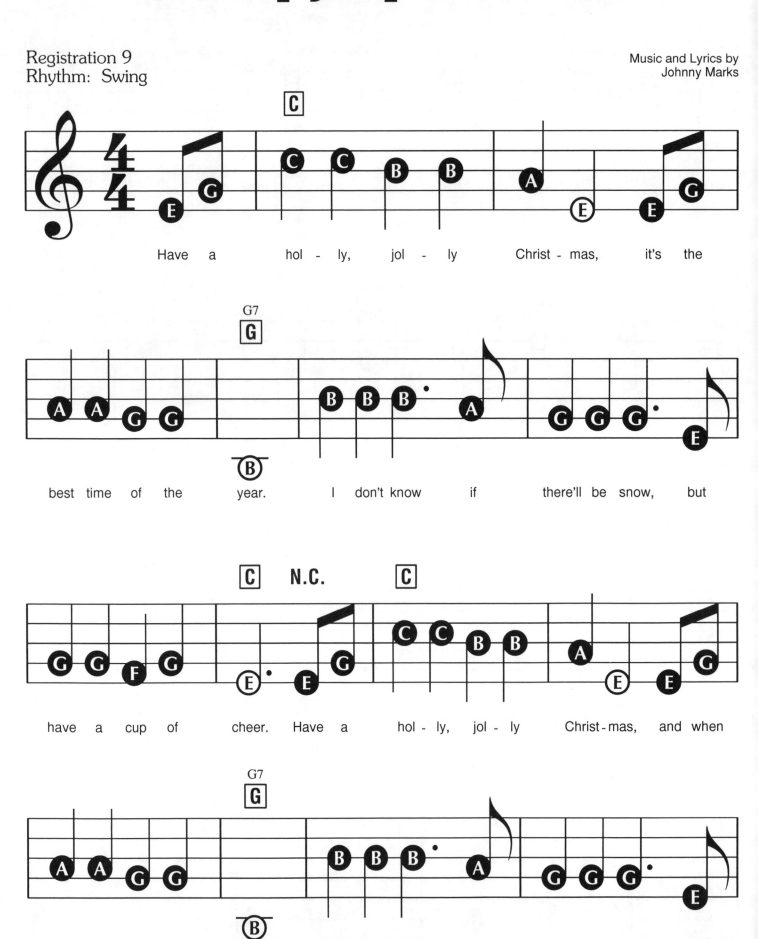

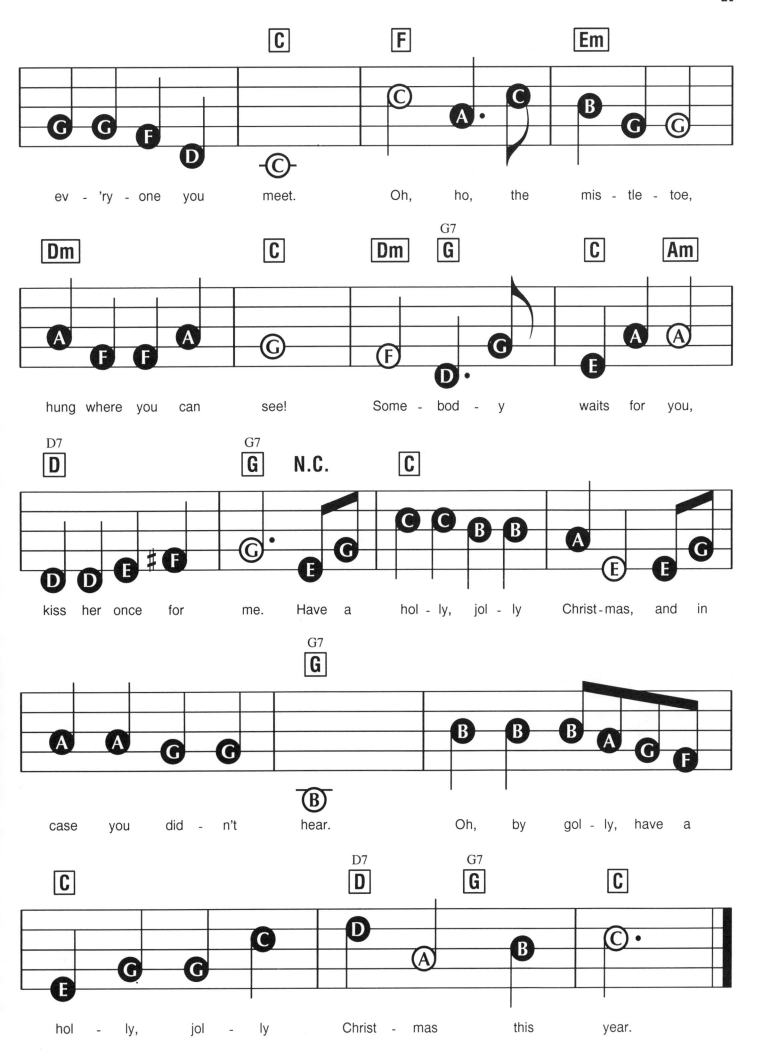

I Heard The Bells On Christmas Day

Registration 9

Words by Henry Longfellow
Adapted by Johnny Marks
Music by Johnny Marks

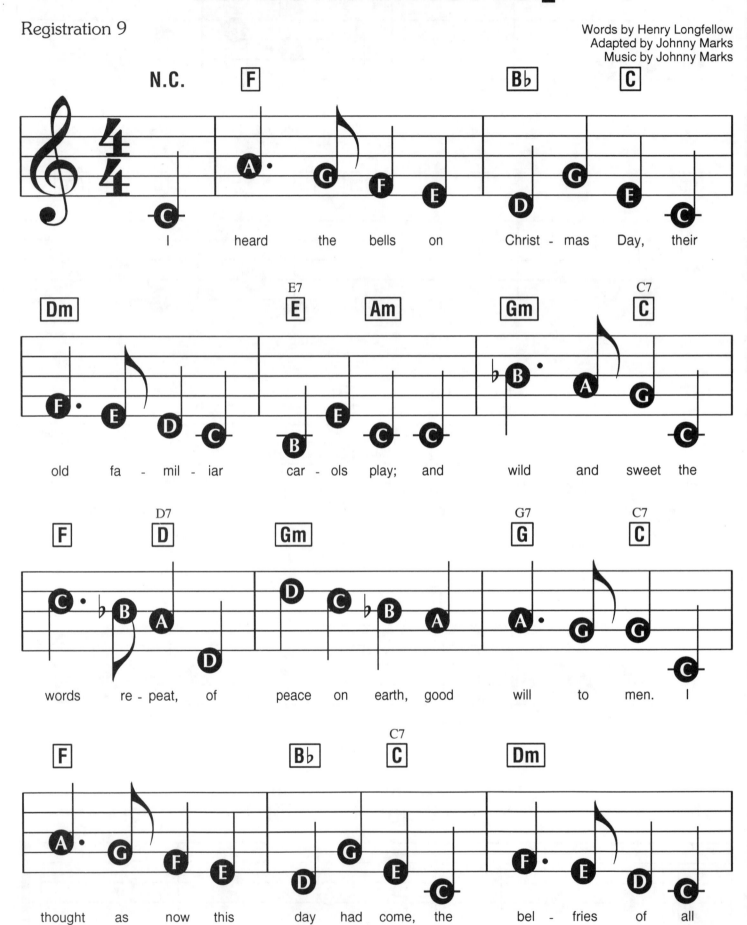

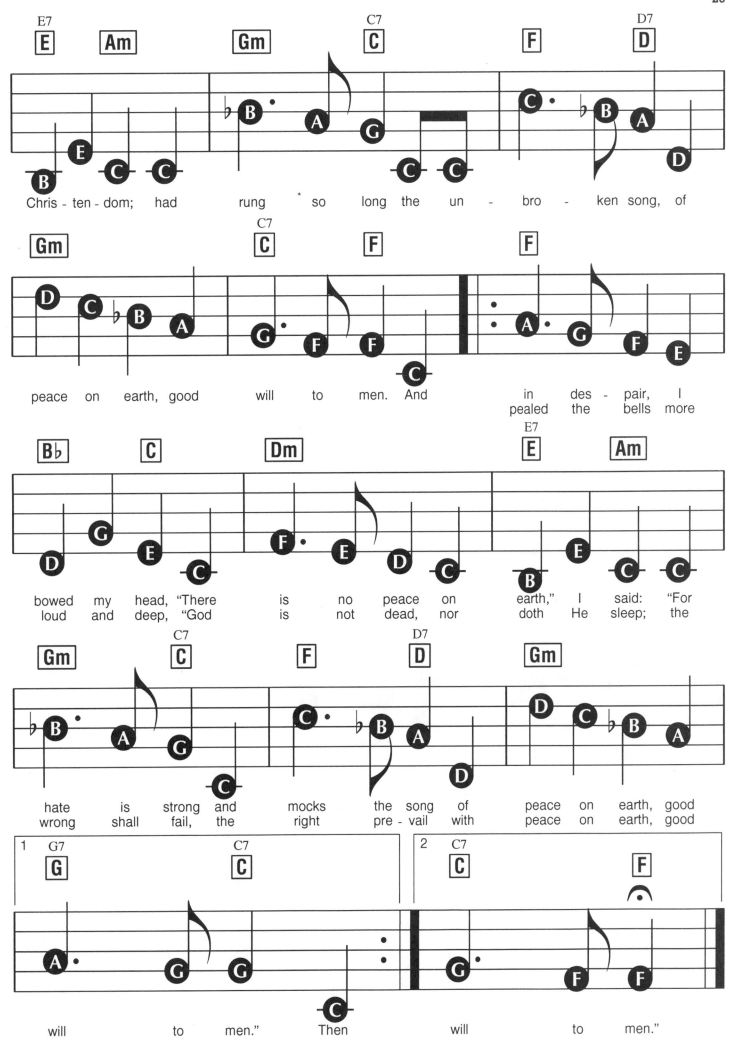

Jingle-Bell Rock

Registration 5
Rhythm: Rock or Fox Trot

Words and Music by Joe Beal
and Jim Boothe

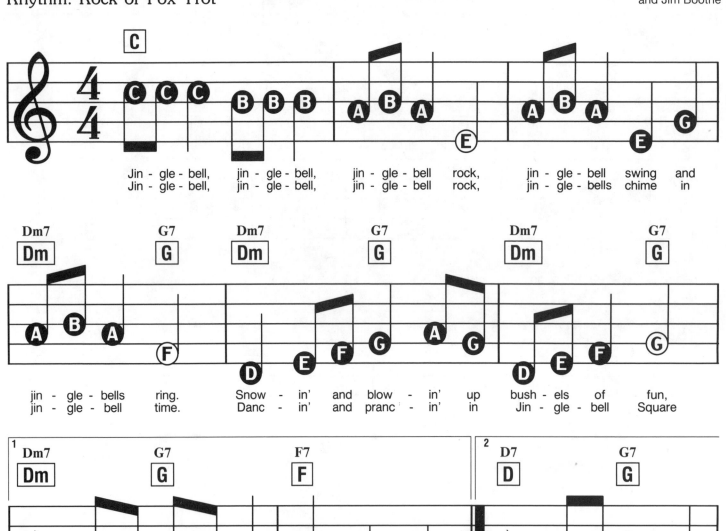

Jin - gle - bell, jin - gle - bell, jin - gle - bell rock, jin - gle - bell swing and
Jin - gle - bell, jin - gle - bell, jin - gle - bell rock, jin - gle - bells chime in

jin - gle - bells ring. Snow - in' and blow - in' up bush - els of fun,
jin - gle - bell time. Danc - in' and pranc - in' in Jin - gle - bell Square

now the jin - gle - hop has be - gun.   in the frost - y

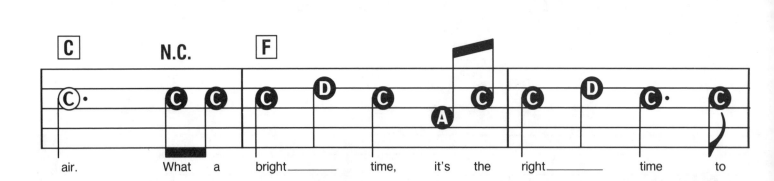

air. What a bright_____ time, it's the right_____ time to

LYRICS FOR
Singalong Christmas Favorites

LUE CHRISTMAS

ll have a blue Christmas
  without you.
ll be so blue thinking about you.
ecorations of red on a green
  Christmas tree,
on't mean a thing if you're not
  here with me.
ll have a blue Christmas, that's
  certain.
nd when that blue heartache
  starts hurtin',
ou'll be doin' all right, with your
  Christmas of white.
ut I'll have a blue, blue Christmas.

ECK THE HALL

eck the hall with boughs of holly,
  fa la la la la, la la la la.
is the season to be jolly,
  fa la la la la, la la la la.

on we now our gay apparel,
  fa la la la la la, la la la la.
roll the ancient Yuletide carol,
  fa la la la la, la la la la.

ee the blazing yule before us,
  fa la la la la, la la la la.
trike the harp and join the chorus,
  fa la la la la, la la la la.

ollow me in merry measure,
  fa la la la la la, la la la la.
Vhile I tell of Yuletide treasure,
  fa la la la la, la la la la.

ast away the old year passes,
  fa la la la la, la la la la.
ail the new, ye lads and lasses,
  fa la la la la, la la la la.

ing we joyous, all together,
  fa la la la la la, la la la la.
eedless of the wind and weather,
  fa la la la la, la la la la.

FROSTY THE SNOW MAN

1. Frosty, the snow man was a jolly
     happy soul,
   with a corn cob pipe and a button
     nose and two eyes made out of
     coal.
   Frosty, the snow man is a fairy
     tale they say,
   he was made of snow but the
     children know how he came to
     life one day.

   There must have been some magic
     in that old silk hat they found.
   For when they placed it on his
     head he began to dance around.
   Oh, Frosty the snow man was
     alive as he could be,
   and the children say he could laugh
     and play just the same as you
     and me.

2. Frosty, the snow man knew the sun
     was hot that day,
   so he said, "Let's run and we'll
     have some fun now before I melt
     away."
   Down to the village, with a
     broomstick in his hand,
   running here and there all around
     the square sayin', "Catch
     me if you can."

   He led them down the streets of
     town right to the traffic cop.
   And he only paused a moment
     when he heard him holler "Stop!"
   For Frosty the snow man had to
     hurry on his way,
   but he waved goodbye sayin',
     "Don't you cry, I'll be back
     again some day."

   Thumpety thump thump, thumpety
     thump thump look at Frosty go.
   Thumpety thump thump, thumpety
     thump thump over the hills of
     snow.

HAPPY HOLIDAY

Happy holiday, happy holiday.
While the merry bells keep ringing,
may your ev'ry wish come true.

Happy holiday, happy holiday.
May the calendar keep bringing,
happy holidays to you.

Happy holiday, happy holiday.
While the merry bells keep ringing,
may your ev'ry wish come true.

Happy holiday, happy holiday.
May the calendar keep bringing,
happy holidays to you.

HAVE YOURSELF A MERRY LITTLE CHRISTMAS

Have yourself a merry little
  Christmas,
let you heart be light.
Next year all our troubles will be
  out of sight.
Have yourself a merry little
  Christmas,
make your Yuletide gay.
Next year all out troubles will be
  miles away.

Once again as in olden days, happy
  golden days of yore,
faithful friends who were dear to us
  will be near to us once more.

Someday soon we all will be
  together,
if the fates allow.
Until then, we'll have to muddle
  through somehow.
So have yourself a merry little
  Christmas now.

HERE COMES SANTA CLAUS
(Right Down Santa Claus Lane)

1. Here comes Santa Claus!
   Here comes Santa Claus!
   Right down Santa Claus Lane!

   Vixen and Blitzen and all his
     reindeer are pulling on the rein.
   Bells are ringing, children singing,
     all is merry and bright.
   Hang your stockings and say your
     pray'rs.
   'cause Santa Claus comes tonight.

2. Here comes Santa Claus!
   Here comes Santa Claus!
   Right down Santa Claus Lane!

   He's got a bag that is filled with
     toys for the boys and girls again.
   Hear those sleighbells jingle jangle,
     what a beautiful sight.
   Jump in bed, cover up your head,
   'cause Santa Claus comes tonight.

3. Here comes Santa Claus!
   Here comes Santa Claus!
   Right down Santa Claus Lane!

   He doesn't care if your rich or
     poor for he loves you just the
     same.
   Santa knows that we're God's
     children, that makes ev'rything
     right.
   Fill your hearts with a Christmas
     cheer,
   'cause Santa Claus comes tonight.

4. Here comes Santa Claus!
   Here comes Santa Claus!
   Right down Santa Claus Lane!

   He'll come around when the
     chimes ring out.
   then it's Christmas morn again.
   Peace on earth will come to all if
     we just follow the light.
   Let's give thanks to the Lord above,
   'cause Santa Claus comes tonight.

Words and Music by Gene Autry and
Oakley Haldeman
Copyright © 1947 (Renewed)
WESTERN MUSIC PUBLISHING CO.
International Copyright Secured
All Rights Reserved

A HOLLY JOLLY CHRISTMAS

Have a holly, jolly Christmas,
  it's the best time of the year.
I don't know if there'll be snow,
  but have a cup of cheer.

Have a holly, jolly Christmas,
  and when you walk down the
  street,
Say hello to friends you know,
  and ev'ryone you meet.

Oh, ho, the mistletoe, hung where
  you can see!
Somebody waits for you, kiss her
  once for me.

Have a holly, jolly Christmas,
  and in case you didn't hear.
Oh, by golly, have a holly, jolly
  Christmas this year.

Music and Lyrics by Johnny Marks
Copyright © 1962, 1964 (Renewed 1990, 1992)
St. Nicholas Music Inc.,
 1619 Broadway, New York, New York 10019
All Rights Reserved

I HEARD THE BELLS ON CHRISTMAS DAY

I heard the bells on Christmas Day,
  their old familiar carols play;
and wild and sweet the words repeat,
  of peace on earth, good will to men.

I thought as now this day had come,
  the belfries of all Christendom;
had rung so long the unbroken song,
  of peace on earth, good will to men.

And in despair, I bowed my head,
  "There is no peace on earth," I said:
"For hate is strong and mocks the song
  of peace on earth, good will to men."

Then pealed the bells more loud and
  deep, "God is not dead, nor doth
  He sleep;
the wrong shall fail, the right prevail
  with peace on earth, good will to
  men."

Words by Henry Longfellow
Adapted by Johnny Marks
Music by Johnny Marks
Copyright © 1956 (Renewed 1984)
St. Nicholas Music Inc.,
 1619 Broadway, New York, New York 10019
All Rights Reserved

JINGLE BELLS

1. Dashing through the snow, in a
     one horse open sleigh,
   o'er the fields we go, laughing all
     the way.
   Bells on bobtail ring, making
     spirits bright,
   what fun it is to ride and sing a
     sleighing song tonight!

   Jingle bells, jingle bells, jingle all
     the way.
   Oh, what fun it is to ride in a
     one horse open sleigh!
   Jingle bells, jingle bells, jingle all
     the way.
   Oh, what fun it is to ride in a
     one horse open sleigh!

2. A day or two ago I thought I'd take
     a ride,
   and soon Miss Fannie Bright was
     seated by my side.
   The horse was lean and lank,
     Miss fortune seemed his lot,
   he got into a drifted bank and
     we, we got upsot!

   Jingle bells, jingle bells, jingle all
     the way.
   Oh, what fun it is to ride in a
     one horse open sleigh!
   Jingle bells, jingle bells, jingle all
     the way.
   Oh, what fun it is to ride in a
     one horse open sleigh!

3. Now the ground is white, go it
     while you're young.
   Take the girls tonight and sing this
     sleighing song.
   Just get a bobtail bay, two-forty
     for his speed.
   then hitch him to an open sleigh
     and crack!
   you'll take the lead.

   Jingle bells, jingle bells, jingle all
     the way.
   Oh, what fun it is to ride in a
     one horse open sleigh!
   Jingle bells, jingle bells, jingle all
     the way.
   Oh, what fun it is to ride in a
     one horse open sleigh!

Words and Music by J. Pierpont
Copyright © 1995 by
HAL LEONARD CORPORATION
International Copyright Secured
All Rights Reserved

LYRICS FOR
Singalong Christmas Favorites

BLUE CHRISTMAS

I'll have a blue Christmas
 without you.
I'll be so blue thinking about you.
Decorations of red on a green
 Christmas tree,
won't mean a thing if you're not
 here with me.
I'll have a blue Christmas, that's
 certain.
And when that blue heartache
 starts hurtin',
you'll be doin' all right, with your
 Christmas of white.
But I'll have a blue, blue Christmas.

DECK THE HALL

Deck the hall with boughs of holly,
 fa la la la la, la la la la.
Tis the season to be jolly,
 fa la la la la, la la la la.

Don we now our gay apparel,
 fa la la la la la, la la la.
Troll the ancient Yuletide carol,
 fa la la la la, la la la la.

See the blazing yule before us,
 fa la la la la, la la la la.
Strike the harp and join the chorus,
 fa la la la la, la la la la.

Follow me in merry measure,
 fa la la la la la, la la la.
While I tell of Yuletide treasure,
 fa la la la la, la la la la.

Fast away the old year passes,
 fa la la la la, la la la la.
Hail the new, ye lads and lasses,
 fa la la la la, la la la la.

Sing we joyous, all together,
 fa la la la la la, la la la.
Heedless of the wind and weather,
 fa la la la la, la la la la.

FROSTY THE SNOW MAN

1. Frosty, the snow man was a jolly
 happy soul,
 with a corn cob pipe and a button
 nose and two eyes made out of
 coal.
 Frosty, the snow man is a fairy
 tale they say,
 he was made of snow but the
 children know how he came to
 life one day.

 There must have been some magic
 in that old silk hat they found.
 For when they placed it on his
 head he began to dance around.
 Oh, Frosty the snow man was
 alive as he could be,
 and the children say he could laugh
 and play just the same as you
 and me.

2. Frosty, the snow man knew the sun
 was hot that day,
 so he said, "Let's run and we'll
 have some fun now before I melt
 away."
 Down to the village, with a
 broomstick in his hand,
 running here and there all around
 the square sayin', "Catch
 me if you can."

 He led them down the streets of
 town right to the traffic cop.
 And he only paused a moment
 when he heard him holler "Stop!"
 For Frosty the snow man had to
 hurry on his way,
 but he waved goodbye sayin',
 "Don't you cry, I'll be back
 again some day."

 Thumpety thump thump, thumpety
 thump thump look at Frosty go.
 Thumpety thump thump, thumpety
 thump thump over the hills of
 snow.

HAPPY HOLIDAY

Happy holiday, happy holiday.
While the merry bells keep ringing,
may your ev'ry wish come true.

Happy holiday, happy holiday.
May the calendar keep bringing,
happy holidays to you.

Happy holiday, happy holiday.
While the merry bells keep ringing,
may your ev'ry wish come true.

Happy holiday, happy holiday.
May the calendar keep bringing,
happy holidays to you.

HAVE YOURSELF A MERRY LITTLE CHRISTMAS

Have yourself a merry little
 Christmas,
let you heart be light.
Next year all our troubles will be
 out of sight.
Have yourself a merry little
 Christmas,
make your Yuletide gay.
Next year all out troubles will be
 miles away.

Once again as in olden days, happy
 golden days of yore,
faithful friends who were dear to us
 will be near to us once more.

Someday soon we all will be
 together,
if the fates allow.
Until then, we'll have to muddle
 through somehow.
So have yourself a merry little
 Christmas now.

HERE COMES SANTA CLAUS
(Right Down Santa Claus Lane)

1. Here comes Santa Claus!
   Here comes Santa Claus!
   Right down Santa Claus Lane!

   Vixen and Blitzen and all his
     reindeer are pulling on the rein.
   Bells are ringing, children singing,
     all is merry and bright.
   Hang your stockings and say your
     pray'rs.
   'cause Santa Claus comes tonight.

2. Here comes Santa Claus!
   Here comes Santa Claus!
   Right down Santa Claus Lane!

   He's got a bag that is filled with
     toys for the boys and girls again.
   Hear those sleighbells jingle jangle,
     what a beautiful sight.
   Jump in bed, cover up your head,
   'cause Santa Claus comes tonight.

3. Here comes Santa Claus!
   Here comes Santa Claus!
   Right down Santa Claus Lane!

   He doesn't care if your rich or
     poor for he loves you just the
     same.
   Santa knows that we're God's
     children, that makes ev'rything
     right.
   Fill your hearts with a Christmas
     cheer,
   'cause Santa Claus comes tonight.

4. Here comes Santa Claus!
   Here comes Santa Claus!
   Right down Santa Claus Lane!

   He'll come around when the
     chimes ring out.
   then it's Christmas morn again.
   Peace on earth will come to all if
     we just follow the light.
   Let's give thanks to the Lord above,
   'cause Santa Claus comes tonight.

Words and Music by Gene Autry and
Oakley Haldeman
Copyright © 1947 (Renewed)
WESTERN MUSIC PUBLISHING CO.
International Copyright Secured
All Rights Reserved

A HOLLY JOLLY CHRISTMAS

Have a holly, jolly Christmas,
  it's the best time of the year.
I don't know if there'll be snow,
  but have a cup of cheer.

Have a holly, jolly Christmas,
  and when you walk down the
  street,
Say hello to friends you know,
  and ev'ryone you meet.

Oh, ho, the mistletoe, hung where
  you can see!
Somebody waits for you, kiss her
  once for me.

Have a holly, jolly Christmas,
  and in case you didn't hear.
Oh, by golly, have a holly, jolly
  Christmas this year.

Music and Lyrics by Johnny Marks
Copyright © 1962, 1964 (Renewed 1990, 1992)
St. Nicholas Music Inc.,
 1619 Broadway, New York, New York 10019
All Rights Reserved

I HEARD THE BELLS ON CHRISTMAS DAY

I heard the bells on Christmas Day,
  their old familiar carols play;
and wild and sweet the words repeat,
  of peace on earth, good will to men.

I thought as now this day had come,
  the belfries of all Christendom;
had rung so long the unbroken song,
  of peace on earth, good will to men.

And in despair, I bowed my head,
  "There is no peace on earth," I said:
"For hate is strong and mocks the song
  of peace on earth, good will to men."

Then pealed the bells more loud and
  deep, "God is not dead, nor doth
  He sleep;
the wrong shall fail, the right prevail
  with peace on earth, good will to
  men."

Words by Henry Longfellow
Adapted by Johnny Marks
Music by Johnny Marks
Copyright © 1956 (Renewed 1984)
St. Nicholas Music Inc.,
 1619 Broadway, New York, New York 10019
All Rights Reserved

JINGLE BELLS

1. Dashing through the snow, in a
     one horse open sleigh,
   o'er the fields we go, laughing all
     the way.
   Bells on bobtail ring, making
     spirits bright,
   what fun it is to ride and sing a
     sleighing song tonight!

   Jingle bells, jingle bells, jingle all
     the way.
   Oh, what fun it is to ride in a
     one horse open sleigh!
   Jingle bells, jingle bells, jingle all
     the way.
   Oh, what fun it is to ride in a
     one horse open sleigh!

2. A day or two ago I thought I'd take
     a ride,
   and soon Miss Fannie Bright was
     seated by my side.
   The horse was lean and lank,
     Miss fortune seemed his lot,
   he got into a drifted bank and
     we, we got upsot!

   Jingle bells, jingle bells, jingle all
     the way.
   Oh, what fun it is to ride in a
     one horse open sleigh!
   Jingle bells, jingle bells, jingle all
     the way.
   Oh, what fun it is to ride in a
     one horse open sleigh!

3. Now the ground is white, go it
     while you're young.
   Take the girls tonight and sing this
     sleighing song.
   Just get a bobtail bay, two-forty
     for his speed.
   then hitch him to an open sleigh
     and crack!
   you'll take the lead.

   Jingle bells, jingle bells, jingle all
     the way.
   Oh, what fun it is to ride in a
     one horse open sleigh!
   Jingle bells, jingle bells, jingle all
     the way.
   Oh, what fun it is to ride in a
     one horse open sleigh!

Words and Music by J. Pierpont
Copyright © 1995 by
HAL LEONARD CORPORATION
International Copyright Secured
All Rights Reserved

LYRICS FOR
Singalong Christmas Favorites

BLUE CHRISTMAS

'll have a blue Christmas
   without you.
'll be so blue thinking about you.
Decorations of red on a green
   Christmas tree,
won't mean a thing if you're not
   here with me.
'll have a blue Christmas, that's
   certain.
And when that blue heartache
   starts hurtin',
you'll be doin' all right, with your
   Christmas of white.
But I'll have a blue, blue Christmas.

DECK THE HALL

Deck the hall with boughs of holly,
   fa la la la la, la la la la.
Tis the season to be jolly,
   fa la la la la, la la la la.

Don we now our gay apparel,
   fa la la la la la, la la la la.
Troll the ancient Yuletide carol,
   fa la la la la, la la la la.

See the blazing yule before us,
   fa la la la la, la la la la.
Strike the harp and join the chorus,
   fa la la la la, la la la la.

Follow me in merry measure,
   fa la la la la la, la la la la.
While I tell of Yuletide treasure,
   fa la la la la, la la la la.

Fast away the old year passes,
   fa la la la la, la la la la.
Hail the new, ye lads and lasses,
   fa la la la la, la la la la.

Sing we joyous, all together,
   fa la la la la la, la la la la.
Heedless of the wind and weather,
   fa la la la la, la la la la.

FROSTY THE SNOW MAN

1. Frosty, the snow man was a jolly
   happy soul,
   with a corn cob pipe and a button
   nose and two eyes made out of
   coal.
   Frosty, the snow man is a fairy
   tale they say,
   he was made of snow but the
   children know how he came to
   life one day.

   There must have been some magic
   in that old silk hat they found.
   For when they placed it on his
   head he began to dance around.
   Oh, Frosty the snow man was
   alive as he could be,
   and the children say he could laugh
   and play just the same as you
   and me.

2. Frosty, the snow man knew the sun
   was hot that day,
   so he said, "Let's run and we'll
   have some fun now before I melt
   away."
   Down to the village, with a
   broomstick in his hand,
   running here and there all around
   the square sayin', "Catch
   me if you can."

   He led them down the streets of
   town right to the traffic cop.
   And he only paused a moment
   when he heard him holler "Stop!"
   For Frosty the snow man had to
   hurry on his way,
   but he waved goodbye sayin',
   "Don't you cry, I'll be back
   again some day."

   Thumpety thump thump, thumpety
   thump thump look at Frosty go.
   Thumpety thump thump, thumpety
   thump thump over the hills of
   snow.

HAPPY HOLIDAY

Happy holiday, happy holiday.
While the merry bells keep ringing,
may your ev'ry wish come true.

Happy holiday, happy holiday.
May the calendar keep bringing,
happy holidays to you.

Happy holiday, happy holiday.
While the merry bells keep ringing,
may your ev'ry wish come true.

Happy holiday, happy holiday.
May the calendar keep bringing,
happy holidays to you.

HAVE YOURSELF A MERRY LITTLE CHRISTMAS

Have yourself a merry little
   Christmas,
let you heart be light.
Next year all our troubles will be
   out of sight.
Have yourself a merry little
   Christmas,
make your Yuletide gay.
Next year all out troubles will be
   miles away.

Once again as in olden days, happy
   golden days of yore,
faithful friends who were dear to us
will be near to us once more.

Someday soon we all will be
   together,
if the fates allow.
Until then, we'll have to muddle
   through somehow.
So have yourself a merry little
   Christmas now.

HERE COMES SANTA CLAUS
(Right Down Santa Claus Lane)

1. Here comes Santa Claus!
   Here comes Santa Claus!
   Right down Santa Claus Lane!

   Vixen and Blitzen and all his
     reindeer are pulling on the rein.
   Bells are ringing, children singing,
     all is merry and bright.
   Hang your stockings and say your
     pray'rs.
   'cause Santa Claus comes tonight.

2. Here comes Santa Claus!
   Here comes Santa Claus!
   Right down Santa Claus Lane!

   He's got a bag that is filled with
     toys for the boys and girls again.
   Hear those sleighbells jingle jangle,
     what a beautiful sight.
   Jump in bed, cover up your head,
   'cause Santa Claus comes tonight.

3. Here comes Santa Claus!
   Here comes Santa Claus!
   Right down Santa Claus Lane!

   He doesn't care if your rich or
     poor for he loves you just the
     same.
   Santa knows that we're God's
     children, that makes ev'rything
     right.
   Fill your hearts with a Christmas
     cheer,
   'cause Santa Claus comes tonight.

4. Here comes Santa Claus!
   Here comes Santa Claus!
   Right down Santa Claus Lane!

   He'll come around when the
     chimes ring out.
   then it's Christmas morn again.
   Peace on earth will come to all if
     we just follow the light.
   Let's give thanks to the Lord above,
   'cause Santa Claus comes tonight.

Words and Music by Gene Autry and
Oakley Haldeman
Copyright © 1947 (Renewed)
WESTERN MUSIC PUBLISHING CO.
International Copyright Secured
All Rights Reserved

A HOLLY JOLLY CHRISTMAS

Have a holly, jolly Christmas,
  it's the best time of the year.
I don't know if there'll be snow,
  but have a cup of cheer.

Have a holly, jolly Christmas,
  and when you walk down the
  street,
Say hello to friends you know,
  and ev'ryone you meet.

Oh, ho, the mistletoe, hung where
  you can see!
Somebody waits for you, kiss her
  once for me.

Have a holly, jolly Christmas,
  and in case you didn't hear.
Oh, by golly, have a holly, jolly
  Christmas this year.

Music and Lyrics by Johnny Marks
Copyright © 1962, 1964 (Renewed 1990, 1992)
St. Nicholas Music Inc.,
  1619 Broadway, New York, New York 10019
All Rights Reserved

I HEARD THE BELLS ON CHRISTMAS DAY

I heard the bells on Christmas Day,
  their old familiar carols play;
and wild and sweet the words repeat,
  of peace on earth, good will to men.

I thought as now this day had come,
  the belfries of all Christendom;
had rung so long the unbroken song,
  of peace on earth, good will to men.

And in despair, I bowed my head,
  "There is no peace on earth," I said:
"For hate is strong and mocks the song
  of peace on earth, good will to men."

Then pealed the bells more loud and
  deep, "God is not dead, nor doth
  He sleep;
the wrong shall fail, the right prevail
  with peace on earth, good will to
  men."

Words by Henry Longfellow
Adapted by Johnny Marks
Music by Johnny Marks
Copyright © 1956 (Renewed 1984)
St. Nicholas Music Inc.,
  1619 Broadway, New York, New York 10019
All Rights Reserved

JINGLE BELLS

1. Dashing through the snow, in a
     one horse open sleigh,
   o'er the fields we go, laughing all
     the way.
   Bells on bobtail ring, making
     spirits bright,
   what fun it is to ride and sing a
     sleighing song tonight!

   Jingle bells, jingle bells, jingle all
     the way.
   Oh, what fun it is to ride in a
     one horse open sleigh!
   Jingle bells, jingle bells, jingle all
     the way.
   Oh, what fun it is to ride in a
     one horse open sleigh!

2. A day or two ago I thought I'd take
     a ride,
   and soon Miss Fannie Bright was
     seated by my side.
   The horse was lean and lank,
     Miss fortune seemed his lot,
   he got into a drifted bank and
     we, we got upsot!

   Jingle bells, jingle bells, jingle all
     the way.
   Oh, what fun it is to ride in a
     one horse open sleigh!
   Jingle bells, jingle bells, jingle all
     the way.
   Oh, what fun it is to ride in a
     one horse open sleigh!

3. Now the ground is white, go it
     while you're young.
   Take the girls tonight and sing this
     sleighing song.
   Just get a bobtail bay, two-forty
     for his speed.
   then hitch him to an open sleigh
     and crack!
   you'll take the lead.

   Jingle bells, jingle bells, jingle all
     the way.
   Oh, what fun it is to ride in a
     one horse open sleigh!
   Jingle bells, jingle bells, jingle all
     the way.
   Oh, what fun it is to ride in a
     one horse open sleigh!

Words and Music by J. Pierpont
Copyright © 1995 by
HAL LEONARD CORPORATION
International Copyright Secured
All Rights Reserved

Singalong Christmas Favorites

BLUE CHRISTMAS

I'll have a blue Christmas
  without you.
I'll be so blue thinking about you.
Decorations of red on a green
  Christmas tree,
won't mean a thing if you're not
  here with me.
I'll have a blue Christmas, that's
  certain.
And when that blue heartache
  starts hurtin',
you'll be doin' all right, with your
  Christmas of white.
But I'll have a blue, blue Christmas.

DECK THE HALL

Deck the hall with boughs of holly,
  fa la la la la, la la la la.
Tis the season to be jolly,
  fa la la la la, la la la la.

Don we now our gay apparel,
  fa la la la la la, la la la la.
Troll the ancient Yuletide carol,
  fa la la la la, la la la la.

See the blazing yule before us,
  fa la la la la, la la la la.
Strike the harp and join the chorus,
  fa la la la la, la la la la.

Follow me in merry measure,
  fa la la la la la, la la la la.
While I tell of Yuletide treasure,
  fa la la la la, la la la la.

Fast away the old year passes,
  fa la la la la, la la la la.
Hail the new, ye lads and lasses,
  fa la la la la, la la la la.

Sing we joyous, all together,
  fa la la la la la, la la la la.
Heedless of the wind and weather,
  fa la la la la, la la la la.

FROSTY THE SNOW MAN

1. Frosty, the snow man was a jolly
   happy soul,
  with a corn cob pipe and a button
   nose and two eyes made out of
   coal.
  Frosty, the snow man is a fairy
   tale they say,
  he was made of snow but the
   children know how he came to
   life one day.

  There must have been some magic
   in that old silk hat they found.
  For when they placed it on his
   head he began to dance around.
  Oh, Frosty the snow man was
   alive as he could be,
  and the children say he could laugh
   and play just the same as you
   and me.

2. Frosty, the snow man knew the sun
   was hot that day,
  so he said, "Let's run and we'll
   have some fun now before I melt
   away."
  Down to the village, with a
   broomstick in his hand,
  running here and there all around
   the square sayin', "Catch
   me if you can."

  He led them down the streets of
   town right to the traffic cop.
  And he only paused a moment
   when he heard him holler "Stop!"
  For Frosty the snow man had to
   hurry on his way,
  but he waved goodbye sayin',
   "Don't you cry, I'll be back
   again some day."

  Thumpety thump thump, thumpety
   thump thump look at Frosty go.
  Thumpety thump thump, thumpety
   thump thump over the hills of
   snow.

HAPPY HOLIDAY

Happy holiday, happy holiday.
While the merry bells keep ringing,
may your ev'ry wish come true.

Happy holiday, happy holiday.
May the calendar keep bringing,
happy holidays to you.

Happy holiday, happy holiday.
While the merry bells keep ringing,
may your ev'ry wish come true.

Happy holiday, happy holiday.
May the calendar keep bringing,
happy holidays to you.

HAVE YOURSELF A MERRY LITTLE CHRISTMAS

Have yourself a merry little
  Christmas,
let you heart be light.
Next year all our troubles will be
  out of sight.
Have yourself a merry little
  Christmas,
make your Yuletide gay.
Next year all out troubles will be
  miles away.

Once again as in olden days, happy
  golden days of yore,
faithful friends who were dear to us
  will be near to us once more.

Someday soon we all will be
  together,
if the fates allow.
Until then, we'll have to muddle
  through somehow.
So have yourself a merry little
  Christmas now.

HERE COMES SANTA CLAUS
(Right Down Santa Claus Lane)

1. Here comes Santa Claus!
   Here comes Santa Claus!
   Right down Santa Claus Lane!

   Vixen and Blitzen and all his
      reindeer are pulling on the rein.
   Bells are ringing, children singing,
      all is merry and bright.
   Hang your stockings and say your
      pray'rs.
   'cause Santa Claus comes tonight.

2. Here comes Santa Claus!
   Here comes Santa Claus!
   Right down Santa Claus Lane!

   He's got a bag that is filled with
      toys for the boys and girls again.
   Hear those sleighbells jingle jangle,
      what a beautiful sight.
   Jump in bed, cover up your head,
   'cause Santa Claus comes tonight.

3. Here comes Santa Claus!
   Here comes Santa Claus!
   Right down Santa Claus Lane!

   He doesn't care if your rich or
      poor for he loves you just the
      same.
   Santa knows that we're God's
      children, that makes ev'rything
      right.
   Fill your hearts with a Christmas
      cheer,
   'cause Santa Claus comes tonight.

4. Here comes Santa Claus!
   Here comes Santa Claus!
   Right down Santa Claus Lane!

   He'll come around when the
      chimes ring out.
   then it's Christmas morn again.
   Peace on earth will come to all if
      we just follow the light.
   Let's give thanks to the Lord above,
   'cause Santa Claus comes tonight.

Words and Music by Gene Autry and
Oakley Haldeman
Copyright © 1947 (Renewed)
WESTERN MUSIC PUBLISHING CO.
International Copyright Secured
All Rights Reserved

A HOLLY JOLLY CHRISTMAS

Have a holly, jolly Christmas,
   it's the best time of the year.
I don't know if there'll be snow,
   but have a cup of cheer.

Have a holly, jolly Christmas,
   and when you walk down the
   street,
Say hello to friends you know,
   and ev'ryone you meet.

Oh, ho, the mistletoe, hung where
   you can see!
Somebody waits for you, kiss her
   once for me.

Have a holly, jolly Christmas,
   and in case you didn't hear.
Oh, by golly, have a holly, jolly
   Christmas this year.

Music and Lyrics by Johnny Marks
Copyright © 1962, 1964 (Renewed 1990, 1992)
St. Nicholas Music Inc.,
 1619 Broadway, New York, New York 10019
All Rights Reserved

I HEARD THE BELLS ON CHRISTMAS DAY

I heard the bells on Christmas Day,
   their old familiar carols play;
and wild and sweet the words repeat,
   of peace on earth, good will to men.

I thought as now this day had come,
   the belfries of all Christendom;
had rung so long the unbroken song,
   of peace on earth, good will to men.

And in despair, I bowed my head,
   "There is no peace on earth," I said:
"For hate is strong and mocks the song
   of peace on earth, good will to men."

Then pealed the bells more loud and
   deep, "God is not dead, nor doth
   He sleep;
the wrong shall fail, the right prevail
   with peace on earth, good will to
   men."

Words by Henry Longfellow
Adapted by Johnny Marks
Music by Johnny Marks
Copyright © 1956 (Renewed 1984)
St. Nicholas Music Inc.,
 1619 Broadway, New York, New York 10019
All Rights Reserved

JINGLE BELLS

1. Dashing through the snow, in a
      one horse open sleigh,
   o'er the fields we go, laughing all
      the way.
   Bells on bobtail ring, making
      spirits bright,
   what fun it is to ride and sing a
      sleighing song tonight!

   Jingle bells, jingle bells, jingle all
      the way.
   Oh, what fun it is to ride in a
      one horse open sleigh!
   Jingle bells, jingle bells, jingle all
      the way.
   Oh, what fun it is to ride in a
      one horse open sleigh!

2. A day or two ago I thought I'd take
      a ride,
   and soon Miss Fannie Bright was
      seated by my side.
   The horse was lean and lank,
      Miss fortune seemed his lot,
   he got into a drifted bank and
      we, we got upsot!

   Jingle bells, jingle bells, jingle all
      the way.
   Oh, what fun it is to ride in a
      one horse open sleigh!
   Jingle bells, jingle bells, jingle all
      the way.
   Oh, what fun it is to ride in a
      one horse open sleigh!

3. Now the ground is white, go it
      while you're young.
   Take the girls tonight and sing this
      sleighing song.
   Just get a bobtail bay, two-forty
      for his speed.
   then hitch him to an open sleigh
      and crack!
   you'll take the lead.

   Jingle bells, jingle bells, jingle all
      the way.
   Oh, what fun it is to ride in a
      one horse open sleigh!
   Jingle bells, jingle bells, jingle all
      the way.
   Oh, what fun it is to ride in a
      one horse open sleigh!

Words and Music by J. Pierpont
Copyright © 1995 by
HAL LEONARD CORPORATION
International Copyright Secured
All Rights Reserved

LYRICS FOR
Singalong Christmas Favorites

BLUE CHRISTMAS

I'll have a blue Christmas
   without you.
I'll be so blue thinking about you.
Decorations of red on a green
   Christmas tree,
won't mean a thing if you're not
   here with me.
I'll have a blue Christmas, that's
   certain.
And when that blue heartache
   starts hurtin',
you'll be doin' all right, with your
   Christmas of white.
But I'll have a blue, blue Christmas.

DECK THE HALL

Deck the hall with boughs of holly,
   fa la la la la, la la la la.
'Tis the season to be jolly,
   fa la la la la, la la la la.

Don we now our gay apparel,
   fa la la la la la, la la la la.
Troll the ancient Yuletide carol,
   fa la la la la, la la la la.

See the blazing yule before us,
   fa la la la la, la la la la.
Strike the harp and join the chorus,
   fa la la la la, la la la la.

Follow me in merry measure,
   fa la la la la la, la la la la.
While I tell of Yuletide treasure,
   fa la la la la la, la la la la.

Fast away the old year passes,
   fa la la la la, la la la la.
Hail the new, ye lads and lasses,
   fa la la la la, la la la la.

Sing we joyous, all together,
   fa la la la la la, la la la la.
Heedless of the wind and weather,
   fa la la la la, la la la la.

FROSTY THE SNOW MAN

1. Frosty, the snow man was a jolly
   happy soul,
   with a corn cob pipe and a button
   nose and two eyes made out of
   coal.
   Frosty, the snow man is a fairy
   tale they say,
   he was made of snow but the
   children know how he came to
   life one day.

   There must have been some magic
   in that old silk hat they found.
   For when they placed it on his
   head he began to dance around.
   Oh, Frosty the snow man was
   alive as he could be,
   and the children say he could laugh
   and play just the same as you
   and me.

2. Frosty, the snow man knew the sun
   was hot that day,
   so he said, "Let's run and we'll
   have some fun now before I melt
   away."
   Down to the village, with a
   broomstick in his hand,
   running here and there all around
   the square sayin', "Catch
   me if you can."

   He led them down the streets of
   town right to the traffic cop.
   And he only paused a moment
   when he heard him holler "Stop!"
   For Frosty the snow man had to
   hurry on his way,
   but he waved goodbye sayin',
   "Don't you cry, I'll be back
   again some day."

   Thumpety thump thump, thumpety
   thump thump look at Frosty go.
   Thumpety thump thump, thumpety
   thump thump over the hills of
   snow.

HAPPY HOLIDAY

Happy holiday, happy holiday.
While the merry bells keep ringing,
may your ev'ry wish come true.

Happy holiday, happy holiday.
May the calendar keep bringing,
happy holidays to you.

Happy holiday, happy holiday.
While the merry bells keep ringing,
may your ev'ry wish come true.

Happy holiday, happy holiday.
May the calendar keep bringing,
happy holidays to you.

HAVE YOURSELF A MERRY LITTLE CHRISTMAS

Have yourself a merry little
   Christmas,
let you heart be light.
Next year all our troubles will be
   out of sight.
Have yourself a merry little
   Christmas,
make your Yuletide gay.
Next year all out troubles will be
   miles away.

Once again as in olden days, happy
   golden days of yore,
faithful friends who were dear to us
   will be near to us once more.

Someday soon we all will be
   together,
if the fates allow.
Until then, we'll have to muddle
   through somehow.
So have yourself a merry little
   Christmas now.

HERE COMES SANTA CLAUS
(Right Down Santa Claus Lane)

1. Here comes Santa Claus!
   Here comes Santa Claus!
   Right down Santa Claus Lane!

   Vixen and Blitzen and all his
     reindeer are pulling on the rein.
   Bells are ringing, children singing,
     all is merry and bright.
   Hang your stockings and say your
     pray'rs.
   'cause Santa Claus comes tonight.

2. Here comes Santa Claus!
   Here comes Santa Claus!
   Right down Santa Claus Lane!

   He's got a bag that is filled with
     toys for the boys and girls again.
   Hear those sleighbells jingle jangle,
     what a beautiful sight.
   Jump in bed, cover up your head,
   'cause Santa Claus comes tonight.

3. Here comes Santa Claus!
   Here comes Santa Claus!
   Right down Santa Claus Lane!

   He doesn't care if your rich or
     poor for he loves you just the
     same.
   Santa knows that we're God's
     children, that makes ev'rything
     right.
   Fill your hearts with a Christmas
     cheer,
   'cause Santa Claus comes tonight.

4. Here comes Santa Claus!
   Here comes Santa Claus!
   Right down Santa Claus Lane!

   He'll come around when the
     chimes ring out.
   then it's Christmas morn again.
   Peace on earth will come to all if
     we just follow the light.
   Let's give thanks to the Lord above,
   'cause Santa Claus comes tonight.

A HOLLY JOLLY CHRISTMAS

Have a holly, jolly Christmas,
  it's the best time of the year.
I don't know if there'll be snow,
  but have a cup of cheer.

Have a holly, jolly Christmas,
  and when you walk down the
  street,
Say hello to friends you know,
  and ev'ryone you meet.

Oh, ho, the mistletoe, hung where
  you can see!
Somebody waits for you, kiss her
  once for me.

Have a holly, jolly Christmas,
  and in case you didn't hear.
Oh, by golly, have a holly, jolly
  Christmas this year.

I HEARD THE BELLS ON CHRISTMAS DAY

I heard the bells on Christmas Day,
  their old familiar carols play;
and wild and sweet the words repeat,
  of peace on earth, good will to men.

I thought as now this day had come,
  the belfries of all Christendom;
had rung so long the unbroken song,
  of peace on earth, good will to men.

And in despair, I bowed my head,
  "There is no peace on earth," I said:
"For hate is strong and mocks the song
  of peace on earth, good will to men."

Then pealed the bells more loud and
  deep, "God is not dead, nor doth
  He sleep;
the wrong shall fail, the right prevail
  with peace on earth, good will to
  men."

JINGLE BELLS

1. Dashing through the snow, in a
     one horse open sleigh,
   o'er the fields we go, laughing all
     the way.
   Bells on bobtail ring, making
     spirits bright,
   what fun it is to ride and sing a
     sleighing song tonight!

   Jingle bells, jingle bells, jingle all
     the way.
   Oh, what fun it is to ride in a
     one horse open sleigh!
   Jingle bells, jingle bells, jingle all
     the way.
   Oh, what fun it is to ride in a
     one horse open sleigh!

2. A day or two ago I thought I'd take
     a ride,
   and soon Miss Fannie Bright was
     seated by my side.
   The horse was lean and lank,
     Miss fortune seemed his lot,
   he got into a drifted bank and
     we, we got upsot!

   Jingle bells, jingle bells, jingle all
     the way.
   Oh, what fun it is to ride in a
     one horse open sleigh!
   Jingle bells, jingle bells, jingle all
     the way.
   Oh, what fun it is to ride in a
     one horse open sleigh!

3. Now the ground is white, go it
     while you're young.
   Take the girls tonight and sing this
     sleighing song.
   Just get a bobtail bay, two-forty
     for his speed.
   then hitch him to an open sleigh
     and crack!
   you'll take the lead.

   Jingle bells, jingle bells, jingle all
     the way.
   Oh, what fun it is to ride in a
     one horse open sleigh!
   Jingle bells, jingle bells, jingle all
     the way.
   Oh, what fun it is to ride in a
     one horse open sleigh!

LYRICS FOR
Singalong Christmas Favorites

BLUE CHRISTMAS

I'll have a blue Christmas
   without you.
I'll be so blue thinking about you.
Decorations of red on a green
   Christmas tree,
won't mean a thing if you're not
   here with me.
I'll have a blue Christmas, that's
   certain.
And when that blue heartache
   starts hurtin',
you'll be doin' all right, with your
   Christmas of white.
But I'll have a blue, blue Christmas.

DECK THE HALL

Deck the hall with boughs of holly,
   fa la la la la, la la la la.
Tis the season to be jolly,
   fa la la la la, la la la la.

Don we now our gay apparel,
   fa la la la la la, la la la.
Troll the ancient Yuletide carol,
   fa la la la la, la la la la.

See the blazing yule before us,
   fa la la la la, la la la la.
Strike the harp and join the chorus,
   fa la la la la, la la la la.

Follow me in merry measure,
   fa la la la la la, la la la.
While I tell of Yuletide treasure,
   fa la la la la, la la la la.

Fast away the old year passes,
   fa la la la la, la la la la.
Hail the new, ye lads and lasses,
   fa la la la la, la la la la.

Sing we joyous, all together,
   fa la la la la la, la la la.
Heedless of the wind and weather,
   fa la la la la, la la la la.

FROSTY THE SNOW MAN

1. Frosty, the snow man was a jolly
   happy soul,
   with a corn cob pipe and a button
   nose and two eyes made out of
   coal.
   Frosty, the snow man is a fairy
   tale they say,
   he was made of snow but the
   children know how he came to
   life one day.

   There must have been some magic
   in that old silk hat they found.
   For when they placed it on his
   head he began to dance around.
   Oh, Frosty the snow man was
   alive as he could be,
   and the children say he could laugh
   and play just the same as you
   and me.

2. Frosty, the snow man knew the sun
   was hot that day,
   so he said, "Let's run and we'll
   have some fun now before I melt
   away."
   Down to the village, with a
   broomstick in his hand,
   running here and there all around
   the square sayin', "Catch
   me if you can."

   He led them down the streets of
   town right to the traffic cop.
   And he only paused a moment
   when he heard him holler "Stop!"
   For Frosty the snow man had to
   hurry on his way,
   but he waved goodbye sayin',
   "Don't you cry, I'll be back
   again some day."

   Thumpety thump thump, thumpety
   thump thump look at Frosty go.
   Thumpety thump thump, thumpety
   thump thump over the hills of
   snow.

HAPPY HOLIDAY

Happy holiday, happy holiday.
While the merry bells keep ringing,
may your ev'ry wish come true.

Happy holiday, happy holiday.
May the calendar keep bringing,
happy holidays to you.

Happy holiday, happy holiday.
While the merry bells keep ringing,
may your ev'ry wish come true.

Happy holiday, happy holiday.
May the calendar keep bringing,
happy holidays to you.

HAVE YOURSELF A MERRY LITTLE CHRISTMAS

Have yourself a merry little
   Christmas,
let you heart be light.
Next year all our troubles will be
   out of sight.
Have yourself a merry little
   Christmas,
make your Yuletide gay.
Next year all out troubles will be
   miles away.

Once again as in olden days, happy
   golden days of yore,
faithful friends who were dear to us
   will be near to us once more.

Someday soon we all will be
   together,
if the fates allow.
Until then, we'll have to muddle
   through somehow.
So have yourself a merry little
   Christmas now.

HERE COMES SANTA CLAUS
(Right Down Santa Claus Lane)

1. Here comes Santa Claus!
   Here comes Santa Claus!
   Right down Santa Claus Lane!

   Vixen and Blitzen and all his
     reindeer are pulling on the rein.
   Bells are ringing, children singing,
     all is merry and bright.
   Hang your stockings and say your
     pray'rs.
   'cause Santa Claus comes tonight.

2. Here comes Santa Claus!
   Here comes Santa Claus!
   Right down Santa Claus Lane!

   He's got a bag that is filled with
     toys for the boys and girls again.
   Hear those sleighbells jingle jangle,
     what a beautiful sight.
   Jump in bed, cover up your head,
   'cause Santa Claus comes tonight.

3. Here comes Santa Claus!
   Here comes Santa Claus!
   Right down Santa Claus Lane!

   He doesn't care if your rich or
     poor for he loves you just the
     same.
   Santa knows that we're God's
     children, that makes ev'rything
     right.
   Fill your hearts with a Christmas
     cheer,
   'cause Santa Claus comes tonight.

4. Here comes Santa Claus!
   Here comes Santa Claus!
   Right down Santa Claus Lane!

   He'll come around when the
     chimes ring out.
   then it's Christmas morn again.
   Peace on earth will come to all if
     we just follow the light.
   Let's give thanks to the Lord above,
   'cause Santa Claus comes tonight.

Words and Music by Gene Autry and
Oakley Haldeman
Copyright © 1947 (Renewed)
WESTERN MUSIC PUBLISHING CO.
International Copyright Secured
All Rights Reserved

A HOLLY JOLLY CHRISTMAS

Have a holly, jolly Christmas,
  it's the best time of the year.
I don't know if there'll be snow,
  but have a cup of cheer.

Have a holly, jolly Christmas,
  and when you walk down the
  street,
Say hello to friends you know,
  and ev'ryone you meet.

Oh, ho, the mistletoe, hung where
  you can see!
Somebody waits for you, kiss her
  once for me.

Have a holly, jolly Christmas,
  and in case you didn't hear.
Oh, by golly, have a holly, jolly
  Christmas this year.

Music and Lyrics by Johnny Marks
Copyright © 1962, 1964 (Renewed 1990, 1992)
St. Nicholas Music Inc.,
  1619 Broadway, New York, New York 10019
All Rights Reserved

I HEARD THE BELLS ON CHRISTMAS DAY

I heard the bells on Christmas Day,
  their old familiar carols play;
and wild and sweet the words repeat,
  of peace on earth, good will to men.

I thought as now this day had come,
  the belfries of all Christendom;
had rung so long the unbroken song,
  of peace on earth, good will to men.

And in despair, I bowed my head,
  "There is no peace on earth," I said:
"For hate is strong and mocks the song
  of peace on earth, good will to men."

Then pealed the bells more loud and
  deep, "God is not dead, nor doth
  He sleep;
the wrong shall fail, the right prevail
  with peace on earth, good will to
  men."

Words by Henry Longfellow
Adapted by Johnny Marks
Music by Johnny Marks
Copyright © 1956 (Renewed 1984)
St. Nicholas Music Inc.,
  1619 Broadway, New York, New York 10019
All Rights Reserved

JINGLE BELLS

1. Dashing through the snow, in a
     one horse open sleigh,
   o'er the fields we go, laughing all
     the way.
   Bells on bobtail ring, making
     spirits bright,
   what fun it is to ride and sing a
     sleighing song tonight!

   Jingle bells, jingle bells, jingle all
     the way.
   Oh, what fun it is to ride in a
     one horse open sleigh!
   Jingle bells, jingle bells, jingle all
     the way.
   Oh, what fun it is to ride in a
     one horse open sleigh!

2. A day or two ago I thought I'd take
     a ride,
   and soon Miss Fannie Bright was
     seated by my side.
   The horse was lean and lank,
     Miss fortune seemed his lot,
   he got into a drifted bank and
     we, we got upsot!

   Jingle bells, jingle bells, jingle all
     the way.
   Oh, what fun it is to ride in a
     one horse open sleigh!
   Jingle bells, jingle bells, jingle all
     the way.
   Oh, what fun it is to ride in a
     one horse open sleigh!

3. Now the ground is white, go it
     while you're young.
   Take the girls tonight and sing this
     sleighing song.
   Just get a bobtail bay, two-forty
     for his speed.
   then hitch him to an open sleigh
     and crack!
   you'll take the lead.

   Jingle bells, jingle bells, jingle all
     the way.
   Oh, what fun it is to ride in a
     one horse open sleigh!
   Jingle bells, jingle bells, jingle all
     the way.
   Oh, what fun it is to ride in a
     one horse open sleigh!

Words and Music by J. Pierpont
Copyright © 1995 by
HAL LEONARD CORPORATION
International Copyright Secured
All Rights Reserved

LYRICS FOR
Singalong Christmas Favorites

BLUE CHRISTMAS

I'll have a blue Christmas
 without you.
I'll be so blue thinking about you.
Decorations of red on a green
 Christmas tree,
won't mean a thing if you're not
 here with me.
I'll have a blue Christmas, that's
 certain.
And when that blue heartache
 starts hurtin',
you'll be doin' all right, with your
 Christmas of white.
But I'll have a blue, blue Christmas.

DECK THE HALL

Deck the hall with boughs of holly,
 fa la la la la, la la la la.
Tis the season to be jolly,
 fa la la la la, la la la la.

Don we now our gay apparel,
 fa la la la la la, la la la.
Troll the ancient Yuletide carol,
 fa la la la la la, la la la la.

See the blazing yule before us,
 fa la la la la, la la la la.
Strike the harp and join the chorus,
 fa la la la la la, la la la la.

Follow me in merry measure,
 fa la la la la la, la la la la.
While I tell of Yuletide treasure,
 fa la la la la la, la la la la.

Fast away the old year passes,
 fa la la la la, la la la la.
Hail the new, ye lads and lasses,
 fa la la la la, la la la la.

Sing we joyous, all together,
 fa la la la la la, la la la la.
Heedless of the wind and weather,
 fa la la la la, la la la la.

FROSTY THE SNOW MAN

1. Frosty, the snow man was a jolly
 happy soul,
 with a corn cob pipe and a button
 nose and two eyes made out of
 coal.
 Frosty, the snow man is a fairy
 tale they say,
 he was made of snow but the
 children know how he came to
 life one day.

 There must have been some magic
 in that old silk hat they found.
 For when they placed it on his
 head he began to dance around.
 Oh, Frosty the snow man was
 alive as he could be,
 and the children say he could laugh
 and play just the same as you
 and me.

2. Frosty, the snow man knew the sun
 was hot that day,
 so he said, "Let's run and we'll
 have some fun now before I melt
 away."
 Down to the village, with a
 broomstick in his hand,
 running here and there all around
 the square sayin', "Catch
 me if you can."

 He led them down the streets of
 town right to the traffic cop.
 And he only paused a moment
 when he heard him holler "Stop!"
 For Frosty the snow man had to
 hurry on his way,
 but he waved goodbye sayin',
 "Don't you cry, I'll be back
 again some day."

 Thumpety thump thump, thumpety
 thump thump look at Frosty go.
 Thumpety thump thump, thumpety
 thump thump over the hills of
 snow.

HAPPY HOLIDAY

Happy holiday, happy holiday.
While the merry bells keep ringing,
may your ev'ry wish come true.

Happy holiday, happy holiday.
May the calendar keep bringing,
happy holidays to you.

Happy holiday, happy holiday.
While the merry bells keep ringing,
may your ev'ry wish come true.

Happy holiday, happy holiday.
May the calendar keep bringing,
happy holidays to you.

HAVE YOURSELF A MERRY LITTLE CHRISTMAS

Have yourself a merry little
 Christmas,
let you heart be light.
Next year all our troubles will be
 out of sight.
Have yourself a merry little
 Christmas,
make your Yuletide gay.
Next year all out troubles will be
 miles away.

Once again as in olden days, happy
 golden days of yore,
faithful friends who were dear to us
 will be near to us once more.

Someday soon we all will be
 together,
if the fates allow.
Until then, we'll have to muddle
 through somehow.
So have yourself a merry little
 Christmas now.

HERE COMES SANTA CLAUS
(Right Down Santa Claus Lane)

1. Here comes Santa Claus!
   Here comes Santa Claus!
   Right down Santa Claus Lane!

   Vixen and Blitzen and all his
      reindeer are pulling on the rein.
   Bells are ringing, children singing,
      all is merry and bright.
   Hang your stockings and say your
      pray'rs.
   'cause Santa Claus comes tonight.

2. Here comes Santa Claus!
   Here comes Santa Claus!
   Right down Santa Claus Lane!

   He's got a bag that is filled with
      toys for the boys and girls again.
   Hear those sleighbells jingle jangle,
      what a beautiful sight.
   Jump in bed, cover up your head,
   'cause Santa Claus comes tonight.

3. Here comes Santa Claus!
   Here comes Santa Claus!
   Right down Santa Claus Lane!

   He doesn't care if your rich or
      poor for he loves you just the
      same.
   Santa knows that we're God's
      children, that makes ev'rything
      right.
   Fill your hearts with a Christmas
      cheer,
   'cause Santa Claus comes tonight.

4. Here comes Santa Claus!
   Here comes Santa Claus!
   Right down Santa Claus Lane!

   He'll come around when the
      chimes ring out.
   then it's Christmas morn again.
   Peace on earth will come to all if
      we just follow the light.
   Let's give thanks to the Lord above,
   'cause Santa Claus comes tonight.

A HOLLY JOLLY CHRISTMAS

Have a holly, jolly Christmas,
   it's the best time of the year.
I don't know if there'll be snow,
   but have a cup of cheer.

Have a holly, jolly Christmas,
   and when you walk down the
   street,
Say hello to friends you know,
   and ev'ryone you meet.

Oh, ho, the mistletoe, hung where
   you can see!
Somebody waits for you, kiss her
   once for me.

Have a holly, jolly Christmas,
   and in case you didn't hear.
Oh, by golly, have a holly, jolly
   Christmas this year.

I HEARD THE BELLS ON CHRISTMAS DAY

I heard the bells on Christmas Day,
   their old familiar carols play;
and wild and sweet the words repeat,
   of peace on earth, good will to men.

I thought as now this day had come,
   the belfries of all Christendom;
had rung so long the unbroken song,
   of peace on earth, good will to men.

And in despair, I bowed my head,
   "There is no peace on earth," I said:
"For hate is strong and mocks the song
   of peace on earth, good will to men."

Then pealed the bells more loud and
   deep, "God is not dead, nor doth
   He sleep;
the wrong shall fail, the right prevail
   with peace on earth, good will to
   men."

JINGLE BELLS

1. Dashing through the snow, in a
      one horse open sleigh,
   o'er the fields we go, laughing all
      the way.
   Bells on bobtail ring, making
      spirits bright,
   what fun it is to ride and sing a
      sleighing song tonight!

   Jingle bells, jingle bells, jingle all
      the way.
   Oh, what fun it is to ride in a
      one horse open sleigh!
   Jingle bells, jingle bells, jingle all
      the way.
   Oh, what fun it is to ride in a
      one horse open sleigh!

2. A day or two ago I thought I'd take
      a ride,
   and soon Miss Fannie Bright was
      seated by my side.
   The horse was lean and lank,
      Miss fortune seemed his lot,
   he got into a drifted bank and
      we, we got upsot!

   Jingle bells, jingle bells, jingle all
      the way.
   Oh, what fun it is to ride in a
      one horse open sleigh!
   Jingle bells, jingle bells, jingle all
      the way.
   Oh, what fun it is to ride in a
      one horse open sleigh!

3. Now the ground is white, go it
      while you're young.
   Take the girls tonight and sing this
      sleighing song.
   Just get a bobtail bay, two-forty
      for his speed.
   then hitch him to an open sleigh
      and crack!
   you'll take the lead.

   Jingle bells, jingle bells, jingle all
      the way.
   Oh, what fun it is to ride in a
      one horse open sleigh!
   Jingle bells, jingle bells, jingle all
      the way.
   Oh, what fun it is to ride in a
      one horse open sleigh!

LYRICS FOR
Singalong Christmas Favorites

BLUE CHRISTMAS

I'll have a blue Christmas
   without you.
I'll be so blue thinking about you.
Decorations of red on a green
   Christmas tree,
won't mean a thing if you're not
   here with me.
I'll have a blue Christmas, that's
   certain.
And when that blue heartache
   starts hurtin',
you'll be doin' all right, with your
   Christmas of white.
But I'll have a blue, blue Christmas.

DECK THE HALL

Deck the hall with boughs of holly,
   fa la la la la, la la la la.
Tis the season to be jolly,
   fa la la la la, la la la la.

Don we now our gay apparel,
   fa la la la la la, la la la.
Troll the ancient Yuletide carol,
   fa la la la la, la la la la.

See the blazing yule before us,
   fa la la la la, la la la la.
Strike the harp and join the chorus,
   fa la la la la, la la la la.

Follow me in merry measure,
   fa la la la la la, la la la.
While I tell of Yuletide treasure,
   fa la la la la, la la la la.

Fast away the old year passes,
   fa la la la la, la la la la.
Hail the new, ye lads and lasses,
   fa la la la la, la la la la.

Sing we joyous, all together,
   fa la la la la la, la la la.
Heedless of the wind and weather,
   fa la la la la, la la la la.

FROSTY THE SNOW MAN

1. Frosty, the snow man was a jolly
   happy soul,
with a corn cob pipe and a button
   nose and two eyes made out of
   coal.
Frosty, the snow man is a fairy
   tale they say,
he was made of snow but the
   children know how he came to
   life one day.

There must have been some magic
   in that old silk hat they found.
For when they placed it on his
   head he began to dance around.
Oh, Frosty the snow man was
   alive as he could be,
and the children say he could laugh
   and play just the same as you
   and me.

2. Frosty, the snow man knew the sun
   was hot that day,
so he said, "Let's run and we'll
   have some fun now before I melt
   away."
Down to the village, with a
   broomstick in his hand,
running here and there all around
   the square sayin', "Catch
   me if you can."

He led them down the streets of
   town right to the traffic cop.
And he only paused a moment
   when he heard him holler "Stop!"
For Frosty the snow man had to
   hurry on his way,
but he waved goodbye sayin',
   "Don't you cry, I'll be back
   again some day."

Thumpety thump thump, thumpety
   thump thump look at Frosty go.
Thumpety thump thump, thumpety
   thump thump over the hills of
   snow.

HAPPY HOLIDAY

Happy holiday, happy holiday.
While the merry bells keep ringing,
may your ev'ry wish come true.

Happy holiday, happy holiday.
May the calendar keep bringing,
happy holidays to you.

Happy holiday, happy holiday.
While the merry bells keep ringing,
may your ev'ry wish come true.

Happy holiday, happy holiday.
May the calendar keep bringing,
happy holidays to you.

HAVE YOURSELF A MERRY LITTLE CHRISTMAS

Have yourself a merry little
   Christmas,
let you heart be light.
Next year all our troubles will be
   out of sight.
Have yourself a merry little
   Christmas,
make your Yuletide gay.
Next year all out troubles will be
   miles away.

Once again as in olden days, happy
   golden days of yore,
faithful friends who were dear to us
   will be near to us once more.

Someday soon we all will be
   together,
if the fates allow.
Until then, we'll have to muddle
   through somehow.
So have yourself a merry little
   Christmas now.

HERE COMES SANTA CLAUS
(Right Down Santa Claus Lane)

1. Here comes Santa Claus!
   Here comes Santa Claus!
   Right down Santa Claus Lane!

   Vixen and Blitzen and all his
     reindeer are pulling on the rein.
   Bells are ringing, children singing,
     all is merry and bright.
   Hang your stockings and say your
     pray'rs.
   'cause Santa Claus comes tonight.

2. Here comes Santa Claus!
   Here comes Santa Claus!
   Right down Santa Claus Lane!

   He's got a bag that is filled with
     toys for the boys and girls again.
   Hear those sleighbells jingle jangle,
     what a beautiful sight.
   Jump in bed, cover up your head,
   'cause Santa Claus comes tonight.

3. Here comes Santa Claus!
   Here comes Santa Claus!
   Right down Santa Claus Lane!

   He doesn't care if your rich or
     poor for he loves you just the
     same.
   Santa knows that we're God's
     children, that makes ev'rything
     right.
   Fill your hearts with a Christmas
     cheer,
   'cause Santa Claus comes tonight.

4. Here comes Santa Claus!
   Here comes Santa Claus!
   Right down Santa Claus Lane!

   He'll come around when the
     chimes ring out.
   then it's Christmas morn again.
   Peace on earth will come to all if
     we just follow the light.
   Let's give thanks to the Lord above,
   'cause Santa Claus comes tonight.

A HOLLY JOLLY CHRISTMAS

Have a holly, jolly Christmas,
   it's the best time of the year.
I don't know if there'll be snow,
   but have a cup of cheer.

Have a holly, jolly Christmas,
   and when you walk down the
   street,
Say hello to friends you know,
   and ev'ryone you meet.

Oh, ho, the mistletoe, hung where
   you can see!
Somebody waits for you, kiss her
   once for me.

Have a holly, jolly Christmas,
   and in case you didn't hear.
Oh, by golly, have a holly, jolly
   Christmas this year.

I HEARD THE BELLS ON CHRISTMAS DAY

I heard the bells on Christmas Day,
   their old familiar carols play;
and wild and sweet the words repeat,
   of peace on earth, good will to men.

I thought as now this day had come,
   the belfries of all Christendom;
had rung so long the unbroken song,
   of peace on earth, good will to men.

And in despair, I bowed my head,
   "There is no peace on earth," I said:
"For hate is strong and mocks the song
   of peace on earth, good will to men."

Then pealed the bells more loud and
   deep, "God is not dead, nor doth
   He sleep;
the wrong shall fail, the right prevail
   with peace on earth, good will to
   men."

JINGLE BELLS

1. Dashing through the snow, in a
     one horse open sleigh,
   o'er the fields we go, laughing all
     the way.
   Bells on bobtail ring, making
     spirits bright,
   what fun it is to ride and sing a
     sleighing song tonight!

   Jingle bells, jingle bells, jingle all
     the way.
   Oh, what fun it is to ride in a
     one horse open sleigh!
   Jingle bells, jingle bells, jingle all
     the way.
   Oh, what fun it is to ride in a
     one horse open sleigh!

2. A day or two ago I thought I'd take
     a ride,
   and soon Miss Fannie Bright was
     seated by my side.
   The horse was lean and lank,
     Miss fortune seemed his lot,
   he got into a drifted bank and
     we, we got upsot!

   Jingle bells, jingle bells, jingle all
     the way.
   Oh, what fun it is to ride in a
     one horse open sleigh!
   Jingle bells, jingle bells, jingle all
     the way.
   Oh, what fun it is to ride in a
     one horse open sleigh!

3. Now the ground is white, go it
     while you're young.
   Take the girls tonight and sing this
     sleighing song.
   Just get a bobtail bay, two-forty
     for his speed.
   then hitch him to an open sleigh
     and crack!
   you'll take the lead.

   Jingle bells, jingle bells, jingle all
     the way.
   Oh, what fun it is to ride in a
     one horse open sleigh!
   Jingle bells, jingle bells, jingle all
     the way.
   Oh, what fun it is to ride in a
     one horse open sleigh!

Singalong Christmas Favorites

BLUE CHRISTMAS

I'll have a blue Christmas
   without you.
I'll be so blue thinking about you.
Decorations of red on a green
   Christmas tree,
won't mean a thing if you're not
   here with me.
I'll have a blue Christmas, that's
   certain.
And when that blue heartache
   starts hurtin',
you'll be doin' all right, with your
   Christmas of white.
But I'll have a blue, blue Christmas.

DECK THE HALL

Deck the hall with boughs of holly,
   fa la la la la, la la la la.
Tis the season to be jolly,
   fa la la la la, la la la la.

Don we now our gay apparel,
   fa la la la la la la, la la la.
Troll the ancient Yuletide carol,
   fa la la la la la, la la la la.

See the blazing yule before us,
   fa la la la la la, la la la la.
Strike the harp and join the chorus,
   fa la la la la la, la la la la.

Follow me in merry measure,
   fa la la la la la, la la la la.
While I tell of Yuletide treasure,
   fa la la la la la, la la la la.

Fast away the old year passes,
   fa la la la la la, la la la la.
Hail the new, ye lads and lasses,
   fa la la la la la, la la la la.

Sing we joyous, all together,
   fa la la la la la la, la la la.
Heedless of the wind and weather,
   fa la la la la la, la la la la.

FROSTY THE SNOW MAN

1. Frosty, the snow man was a jolly
   happy soul,
   with a corn cob pipe and a button
     nose and two eyes made out of
     coal.
   Frosty, the snow man is a fairy
     tale they say,
   he was made of snow but the
     children know how he came to
     life one day.

   There must have been some magic
     in that old silk hat they found.
   For when they placed it on his
     head he began to dance around.
   Oh, Frosty the snow man was
     alive as he could be,
   and the children say he could laugh
     and play just the same as you
     and me.

2. Frosty, the snow man knew the sun
   was hot that day,
   so he said, "Let's run and we'll
     have some fun now before I melt
     away."
   Down to the village, with a
     broomstick in his hand,
   running here and there all around
     the square sayin', "Catch
     me if you can."

   He led them down the streets of
     town right to the traffic cop.
   And he only paused a moment
     when he heard him holler "Stop!"
   For Frosty the snow man had to
     hurry on his way,
   but he waved goodbye sayin',
     "Don't you cry, I'll be back
     again some day."

   Thumpety thump thump, thumpety
     thump thump look at Frosty go.
   Thumpety thump thump, thumpety
     thump thump over the hills of
     snow.

HAPPY HOLIDAY

Happy holiday, happy holiday.
While the merry bells keep ringing,
may your ev'ry wish come true.

Happy holiday, happy holiday.
May the calendar keep bringing,
happy holidays to you.

Happy holiday, happy holiday.
While the merry bells keep ringing,
may your ev'ry wish come true.

Happy holiday, happy holiday.
May the calendar keep bringing,
happy holidays to you.

HAVE YOURSELF A MERRY LITTLE CHRISTMAS

Have yourself a merry little
   Christmas,
let you heart be light.
Next year all our troubles will be
   out of sight.
Have yourself a merry little
   Christmas,
make your Yuletide gay.
Next year all out troubles will be
   miles away.

Once again as in olden days, happy
   golden days of yore,
faithful friends who were dear to us
   will be near to us once more.

Someday soon we all will be
   together,
if the fates allow.
Until then, we'll have to muddle
   through somehow.
So have yourself a merry little
   Christmas now.

HERE COMES SANTA CLAUS
(Right Down Santa Claus Lane)

1. Here comes Santa Claus!
   Here comes Santa Claus!
   Right down Santa Claus Lane!

   Vixen and Blitzen and all his
   reindeer are pulling on the rein.
   Bells are ringing, children singing,
   all is merry and bright.
   Hang your stockings and say your
   pray'rs.
   'cause Santa Claus comes tonight.

2. Here comes Santa Claus!
   Here comes Santa Claus!
   Right down Santa Claus Lane!

   He's got a bag that is filled with
   toys for the boys and girls again.
   Hear those sleighbells jingle jangle,
   what a beautiful sight.
   Jump in bed, cover up your head,
   'cause Santa Claus comes tonight.

3. Here comes Santa Claus!
   Here comes Santa Claus!
   Right down Santa Claus Lane!

   He doesn't care if your rich or
   poor for he loves you just the
   same.
   Santa knows that we're God's
   children, that makes ev'rything
   right.
   Fill your hearts with a Christmas
   cheer,
   'cause Santa Claus comes tonight.

4. Here comes Santa Claus!
   Here comes Santa Claus!
   Right down Santa Claus Lane!

   He'll come around when the
   chimes ring out.
   then it's Christmas morn again.
   Peace on earth will come to all if
   we just follow the light.
   Let's give thanks to the Lord above,
   'cause Santa Claus comes tonight.

A HOLLY JOLLY CHRISTMAS

Have a holly, jolly Christmas,
   it's the best time of the year.
I don't know if there'll be snow,
   but have a cup of cheer.

Have a holly, jolly Christmas,
   and when you walk down the
   street,
Say hello to friends you know,
   and ev'ryone you meet.

Oh, ho, the mistletoe, hung where
   you can see!
Somebody waits for you, kiss her
   once for me.

Have a holly, jolly Christmas,
   and in case you didn't hear.
Oh, by golly, have a holly, jolly
   Christmas this year.

I HEARD THE BELLS ON CHRISTMAS DAY

I heard the bells on Christmas Day,
   their old familiar carols play;
and wild and sweet the words repeat,
   of peace on earth, good will to men.

I thought as now this day had come,
   the belfries of all Christendom;
had rung so long the unbroken song,
   of peace on earth, good will to men.

And in despair, I bowed my head,
   "There is no peace on earth," I said:
"For hate is strong and mocks the song
   of peace on earth, good will to men."

Then pealed the bells more loud and
   deep, "God is not dead, nor doth
   He sleep;
the wrong shall fail, the right prevail
   with peace on earth, good will to
   men."

JINGLE BELLS

1. Dashing through the snow, in a
   one horse open sleigh,
   o'er the fields we go, laughing all
   the way.
   Bells on bobtail ring, making
   spirits bright,
   what fun it is to ride and sing a
   sleighing song tonight!

   Jingle bells, jingle bells, jingle all
   the way.
   Oh, what fun it is to ride in a
   one horse open sleigh!
   Jingle bells, jingle bells, jingle all
   the way.
   Oh, what fun it is to ride in a
   one horse open sleigh!

2. A day or two ago I thought I'd take
   a ride,
   and soon Miss Fannie Bright was
   seated by my side.
   The horse was lean and lank,
   Miss fortune seemed his lot,
   he got into a drifted bank and
   we, we got upsot!

   Jingle bells, jingle bells, jingle all
   the way.
   Oh, what fun it is to ride in a
   one horse open sleigh!
   Jingle bells, jingle bells, jingle all
   the way.
   Oh, what fun it is to ride in a
   one horse open sleigh!

3. Now the ground is white, go it
   while you're young.
   Take the girls tonight and sing this
   sleighing song.
   Just get a bobtail bay, two-forty
   for his speed.
   then hitch him to an open sleigh
   and crack!
   you'll take the lead.

   Jingle bells, jingle bells, jingle all
   the way.
   Oh, what fun it is to ride in a
   one horse open sleigh!
   Jingle bells, jingle bells, jingle all
   the way.
   Oh, what fun it is to ride in a
   one horse open sleigh!

LYRICS FOR
Singalong Christmas Favorites

BLUE CHRISTMAS

I'll have a blue Christmas
  without you.
I'll be so blue thinking about you.
Decorations of red on a green
  Christmas tree,
won't mean a thing if you're not
  here with me.
I'll have a blue Christmas, that's
  certain.
And when that blue heartache
  starts hurtin',
you'll be doin' all right, with your
  Christmas of white.
But I'll have a blue, blue Christmas.

DECK THE HALL

Deck the hall with boughs of holly,
  fa la la la la, la la la la.
Tis the season to be jolly,
  fa la la la la, la la la la.

Don we now our gay apparel,
  fa la la la la la, la la la.
Troll the ancient Yuletide carol,
  fa la la la la, la la la la.

See the blazing yule before us,
  fa la la la la, la la la la.
Strike the harp and join the chorus,
  fa la la la la, la la la la.

Follow me in merry measure,
  fa la la la la la, la la la.
While I tell of Yuletide treasure,
  fa la la la la, la la la la.

Fast away the old year passes,
  fa la la la la, la la la la.
Hail the new, ye lads and lasses,
  fa la la la la, la la la la.

Sing we joyous, all together,
  fa la la la la la, la la la.
Heedless of the wind and weather,
  fa la la la la, la la la la.

FROSTY THE SNOW MAN

1. Frosty, the snow man was a jolly
  happy soul,
with a corn cob pipe and a button
  nose and two eyes made out of
  coal.
Frosty, the snow man is a fairy
  tale they say,
he was made of snow but the
  children know how he came to
  life one day.

There must have been some magic
  in that old silk hat they found.
For when they placed it on his
  head he began to dance around.
Oh, Frosty the snow man was
  alive as he could be,
and the children say he could laugh
  and play just the same as you
  and me.

2. Frosty, the snow man knew the sun
  was hot that day,
so he said, "Let's run and we'll
  have some fun now before I melt
  away."
Down to the village, with a
  broomstick in his hand,
running here and there all around
  the square sayin', "Catch
  me if you can."

He led them down the streets of
  town right to the traffic cop.
And he only paused a moment
  when he heard him holler "Stop!"
For Frosty the snow man had to
  hurry on his way,
but he waved goodbye sayin',
  "Don't you cry, I'll be back
  again some day."

Thumpety thump thump, thumpety
  thump thump look at Frosty go.
Thumpety thump thump, thumpety
  thump thump over the hills of
  snow.

HAPPY HOLIDAY

Happy holiday, happy holiday.
While the merry bells keep ringing,
may your ev'ry wish come true.

Happy holiday, happy holiday.
May the calendar keep bringing,
happy holidays to you.

Happy holiday, happy holiday.
While the merry bells keep ringing,
may your ev'ry wish come true.

Happy holiday, happy holiday.
May the calendar keep bringing,
happy holidays to you.

HAVE YOURSELF A MERRY LITTLE CHRISTMAS

Have yourself a merry little
  Christmas,
let you heart be light.
Next year all our troubles will be
  out of sight.
Have yourself a merry little
  Christmas,
make your Yuletide gay.
Next year all out troubles will be
  miles away.

Once again as in olden days, happy
  golden days of yore,
faithful friends who were dear to us
  will be near to us once more.

Someday soon we all will be
  together,
if the fates allow.
Until then, we'll have to muddle
  through somehow.
So have yourself a merry little
  Christmas now.

HERE COMES SANTA CLAUS
(Right Down Santa Claus Lane)

1. Here comes Santa Claus!
   Here comes Santa Claus!
   Right down Santa Claus Lane!

   Vixen and Blitzen and all his
      reindeer are pulling on the rein.
   Bells are ringing, children singing,
      all is merry and bright.
   Hang your stockings and say your
      pray'rs.
   'cause Santa Claus comes tonight.

2. Here comes Santa Claus!
   Here comes Santa Claus!
   Right down Santa Claus Lane!

   He's got a bag that is filled with
      toys for the boys and girls again.
   Hear those sleighbells jingle jangle,
      what a beautiful sight.
   Jump in bed, cover up your head,
   'cause Santa Claus comes tonight.

3. Here comes Santa Claus!
   Here comes Santa Claus!
   Right down Santa Claus Lane!

   He doesn't care if your rich or
      poor for he loves you just the
      same.
   Santa knows that we're God's
      children, that makes ev'rything
      right.
   Fill your hearts with a Christmas
      cheer,
   'cause Santa Claus comes tonight.

4. Here comes Santa Claus!
   Here comes Santa Claus!
   Right down Santa Claus Lane!

   He'll come around when the
      chimes ring out.
   then it's Christmas morn again.
   Peace on earth will come to all if
      we just follow the light.
   Let's give thanks to the Lord above,
   'cause Santa Claus comes tonight.

Words and Music by Gene Autry and
Oakley Haldeman
Copyright © 1947 (Renewed)
WESTERN MUSIC PUBLISHING CO.
International Copyright Secured
All Rights Reserved

A HOLLY JOLLY CHRISTMAS

Have a holly, jolly Christmas,
   it's the best time of the year.
I don't know if there'll be snow,
   but have a cup of cheer.

Have a holly, jolly Christmas,
   and when you walk down the
   street,
Say hello to friends you know,
   and ev'ryone you meet.

Oh, ho, the mistletoe, hung where
   you can see!
Somebody waits for you, kiss her
   once for me.

Have a holly, jolly Christmas,
   and in case you didn't hear.
Oh, by golly, have a holly, jolly
Christmas this year.

Music and Lyrics by Johnny Marks
Copyright © 1962, 1964 (Renewed 1990, 1992)
St. Nicholas Music Inc.,
 1619 Broadway, New York, New York 10019
All Rights Reserved

I HEARD THE BELLS ON CHRISTMAS DAY

I heard the bells on Christmas Day,
   their old familiar carols play;
and wild and sweet the words repeat,
   of peace on earth, good will to men.

I thought as now this day had come,
   the belfries of all Christendom;
had rung so long the unbroken song,
   of peace on earth, good will to men.

And in despair, I bowed my head,
   "There is no peace on earth," I said:
"For hate is strong and mocks the song
   of peace on earth, good will to men."

Then pealed the bells more loud and
   deep, "God is not dead, nor doth
   He sleep;
the wrong shall fail, the right prevail
   with peace on earth, good will to
   men."

Words by Henry Longfellow
Adapted by Johnny Marks
Music by Johnny Marks
Copyright © 1956 (Renewed 1984)
St. Nicholas Music Inc.,
 1619 Broadway, New York, New York 10019
All Rights Reserved

JINGLE BELLS

1. Dashing through the snow, in a
      one horse open sleigh,
   o'er the fields we go, laughing all
      the way.
   Bells on bobtail ring, making
      spirits bright,
   what fun it is to ride and sing a
      sleighing song tonight!

   Jingle bells, jingle bells, jingle all
      the way.
   Oh, what fun it is to ride in a
      one horse open sleigh!
   Jingle bells, jingle bells, jingle all
      the way.
   Oh, what fun it is to ride in a
      one horse open sleigh!

2. A day or two ago I thought I'd take
      a ride,
   and soon Miss Fannie Bright was
      seated by my side.
   The horse was lean and lank,
      Miss fortune seemed his lot,
   he got into a drifted bank and
      we, we got upsot!

   Jingle bells, jingle bells, jingle all
      the way.
   Oh, what fun it is to ride in a
      one horse open sleigh!
   Jingle bells, jingle bells, jingle all
      the way.
   Oh, what fun it is to ride in a
      one horse open sleigh!

3. Now the ground is white, go it
      while you're young.
   Take the girls tonight and sing this
      sleighing song.
   Just get a bobtail bay, two-forty
      for his speed.
   then hitch him to an open sleigh
      and crack!
   you'll take the lead.

   Jingle bells, jingle bells, jingle all
      the way.
   Oh, what fun it is to ride in a
      one horse open sleigh!
   Jingle bells, jingle bells, jingle all
      the way.
   Oh, what fun it is to ride in a
      one horse open sleigh!

Words and Music by J. Pierpont
Copyright © 1995 by
HAL LEONARD CORPORATION
International Copyright Secured
All Rights Reserved

LYRICS FOR
Singalong Christmas Favorites

BLUE CHRISTMAS

I'll have a blue Christmas
  without you.
I'll be so blue thinking about you.
Decorations of red on a green
  Christmas tree,
won't mean a thing if you're not
  here with me.
I'll have a blue Christmas, that's
  certain.
And when that blue heartache
  starts hurtin',
you'll be doin' all right, with your
  Christmas of white.
But I'll have a blue, blue Christmas.

DECK THE HALL

Deck the hall with boughs of holly,
  fa la la la la, la la la la.
Tis the season to be jolly,
  fa la la la la, la la la la.

Don we now our gay apparel,
  fa la la la la la, la la la.
Troll the ancient Yuletide carol,
  fa la la la la la, la la la la.

See the blazing yule before us,
  fa la la la la la, la la la la.
Strike the harp and join the chorus,
  fa la la la la la, la la la la.

Follow me in merry measure,
  fa la la la la la, la la la.
While I tell of Yuletide treasure,
  fa la la la la la, la la la la.

Fast away the old year passes,
  fa la la la la, la la la la.
Hail the new, ye lads and lasses,
  fa la la la la, la la la la.

Sing we joyous, all together,
  fa la la la la la, la la la.
Heedless of the wind and weather,
  fa la la la la, la la la la.

FROSTY THE SNOW MAN

1. Frosty, the snow man was a jolly
    happy soul,
  with a corn cob pipe and a button
    nose and two eyes made out of
    coal.
  Frosty, the snow man is a fairy
    tale they say,
  he was made of snow but the
    children know how he came to
    life one day.

  There must have been some magic
    in that old silk hat they found.
  For when they placed it on his
    head he began to dance around.
  Oh, Frosty the snow man was
    alive as he could be,
  and the children say he could laugh
    and play just the same as you
    and me.

2. Frosty, the snow man knew the sun
    was hot that day,
  so he said, "Let's run and we'll
    have some fun now before I melt
    away."
  Down to the village, with a
    broomstick in his hand,
  running here and there all around
    the square sayin', "Catch
    me if you can."

  He led them down the streets of
    town right to the traffic cop.
  And he only paused a moment
    when he heard him holler "Stop!"
  For Frosty the snow man had to
    hurry on his way,
  but he waved goodbye sayin',
    "Don't you cry, I'll be back
    again some day."

  Thumpety thump thump, thumpety
    thump thump look at Frosty go.
  Thumpety thump thump, thumpety
    thump thump over the hills of
    snow.

HAPPY HOLIDAY

Happy holiday, happy holiday.
While the merry bells keep ringing,
may your ev'ry wish come true.

Happy holiday, happy holiday.
May the calendar keep bringing,
happy holidays to you.

Happy holiday, happy holiday.
While the merry bells keep ringing,
may your ev'ry wish come true.

Happy holiday, happy holiday.
May the calendar keep bringing,
happy holidays to you.

HAVE YOURSELF A MERRY LITTLE CHRISTMAS

Have yourself a merry little
  Christmas,
let you heart be light.
Next year all our troubles will be
  out of sight.
Have yourself a merry little
  Christmas,
make your Yuletide gay.
Next year all out troubles will be
  miles away.

Once again as in olden days, happy
  golden days of yore,
faithful friends who were dear to us
  will be near to us once more.

Someday soon we all will be
  together,
if the fates allow.
Until then, we'll have to muddle
  through somehow.
So have yourself a merry little
  Christmas now.

HERE COMES SANTA CLAUS
(Right Down Santa Claus Lane)

1. Here comes Santa Claus!
   Here comes Santa Claus!
   Right down Santa Claus Lane!

   Vixen and Blitzen and all his
     reindeer are pulling on the rein.
   Bells are ringing, children singing,
     all is merry and bright.
   Hang your stockings and say your
     pray'rs.
   'cause Santa Claus comes tonight.

2. Here comes Santa Claus!
   Here comes Santa Claus!
   Right down Santa Claus Lane!

   He's got a bag that is filled with
     toys for the boys and girls again.
   Hear those sleighbells jingle jangle,
     what a beautiful sight.
   Jump in bed, cover up your head,
   'cause Santa Claus comes tonight.

3. Here comes Santa Claus!
   Here comes Santa Claus!
   Right down Santa Claus Lane!

   He doesn't care if your rich or
     poor for he loves you just the
     same.
   Santa knows that we're God's
     children, that makes ev'rything
     right.
   Fill your hearts with a Christmas
     cheer,
   'cause Santa Claus comes tonight.

4. Here comes Santa Claus!
   Here comes Santa Claus!
   Right down Santa Claus Lane!

   He'll come around when the
     chimes ring out.
   then it's Christmas morn again.
   Peace on earth will come to all if
     we just follow the light.
   Let's give thanks to the Lord above,
   'cause Santa Claus comes tonight.

A HOLLY JOLLY CHRISTMAS

Have a holly, jolly Christmas,
  it's the best time of the year.
I don't know if there'll be snow,
  but have a cup of cheer.

Have a holly, jolly Christmas,
  and when you walk down the
  street,
Say hello to friends you know,
  and ev'ryone you meet.

Oh, ho, the mistletoe, hung where
  you can see!
Somebody waits for you, kiss her
  once for me.

Have a holly, jolly Christmas,
  and in case you didn't hear.
Oh, by golly, have a holly, jolly
  Christmas this year.

I HEARD THE BELLS ON CHRISTMAS DAY

I heard the bells on Christmas Day,
  their old familiar carols play;
and wild and sweet the words repeat,
  of peace on earth, good will to men.

I thought as now this day had come,
  the belfries of all Christendom;
had rung so long the unbroken song,
  of peace on earth, good will to men.

And in despair, I bowed my head,
  "There is no peace on earth," I said:
"For hate is strong and mocks the song
  of peace on earth, good will to men."

Then pealed the bells more loud and
  deep, "God is not dead, nor doth
  He sleep;
the wrong shall fail, the right prevail
  with peace on earth, good will to
  men."

JINGLE BELLS

1. Dashing through the snow, in a
     one horse open sleigh,
   o'er the fields we go, laughing all
     the way.
   Bells on bobtail ring, making
     spirits bright,
   what fun it is to ride and sing a
     sleighing song tonight!

   Jingle bells, jingle bells, jingle all
     the way.
   Oh, what fun it is to ride in a
     one horse open sleigh!
   Jingle bells, jingle bells, jingle all
     the way.
   Oh, what fun it is to ride in a
     one horse open sleigh!

2. A day or two ago I thought I'd take
     a ride,
   and soon Miss Fannie Bright was
     seated by my side.
   The horse was lean and lank,
     Miss fortune seemed his lot,
   he got into a drifted bank and
     we, we got upsot!

   Jingle bells, jingle bells, jingle all
     the way.
   Oh, what fun it is to ride in a
     one horse open sleigh!
   Jingle bells, jingle bells, jingle all
     the way.
   Oh, what fun it is to ride in a
     one horse open sleigh!

3. Now the ground is white, go it
     while you're young.
   Take the girls tonight and sing this
     sleighing song.
   Just get a bobtail bay, two-forty
     for his speed.
   then hitch him to an open sleigh
     and crack!
   you'll take the lead.

   Jingle bells, jingle bells, jingle all
     the way.
   Oh, what fun it is to ride in a
     one horse open sleigh!
   Jingle bells, jingle bells, jingle all
     the way.
   Oh, what fun it is to ride in a
     one horse open sleigh!

LYRICS FOR
Singalong Christmas Favorites

BLUE CHRISTMAS

I'll have a blue Christmas
 without you.
I'll be so blue thinking about you.
Decorations of red on a green
 Christmas tree,
won't mean a thing if you're not
 here with me.
I'll have a blue Christmas, that's
 certain.
And when that blue heartache
 starts hurtin',
you'll be doin' all right, with your
 Christmas of white.
But I'll have a blue, blue Christmas.

DECK THE HALL

Deck the hall with boughs of holly,
 fa la la la la, la la la la.
Tis the season to be jolly,
 fa la la la la, la la la la.

Don we now our gay apparel,
 fa la la la la la, la la la la.
Troll the ancient Yuletide carol,
 fa la la la la, la la la la.

See the blazing yule before us,
 fa la la la la, la la la la.
Strike the harp and join the chorus,
 fa la la la la, la la la la.

Follow me in merry measure,
 fa la la la la la, la la la la.
While I tell of Yuletide treasure,
 fa la la la la, la la la la.

Fast away the old year passes,
 fa la la la la, la la la la.
Hail the new, ye lads and lasses,
 fa la la la la, la la la la.

Sing we joyous, all together,
 fa la la la la la, la la la la.
Heedless of the wind and weather,
 fa la la la la, la la la la.

FROSTY THE SNOW MAN

1. Frosty, the snow man was a jolly
 happy soul,
 with a corn cob pipe and a button
 nose and two eyes made out of
 coal.
 Frosty, the snow man is a fairy
 tale they say,
 he was made of snow but the
 children know how he came to
 life one day.

 There must have been some magic
 in that old silk hat they found.
 For when they placed it on his
 head he began to dance around.
 Oh, Frosty the snow man was
 alive as he could be,
 and the children say he could laugh
 and play just the same as you
 and me.

2. Frosty, the snow man knew the sun
 was hot that day,
 so he said, "Let's run and we'll
 have some fun now before I melt
 away."
 Down to the village, with a
 broomstick in his hand,
 running here and there all around
 the square sayin', "Catch
 me if you can."

 He led them down the streets of
 town right to the traffic cop.
 And he only paused a moment
 when he heard him holler "Stop!"
 For Frosty the snow man had to
 hurry on his way,
 but he waved goodbye sayin',
 "Don't you cry, I'll be back
 again some day."

 Thumpety thump thump, thumpety
 thump thump look at Frosty go.
 Thumpety thump thump, thumpety
 thump thump over the hills of
 snow.

HAPPY HOLIDAY

Happy holiday, happy holiday.
While the merry bells keep ringing,
may your ev'ry wish come true.

Happy holiday, happy holiday.
May the calendar keep bringing,
happy holidays to you.

Happy holiday, happy holiday.
While the merry bells keep ringing,
may your ev'ry wish come true.

Happy holiday, happy holiday.
May the calendar keep bringing,
happy holidays to you.

HAVE YOURSELF A MERRY LITTLE CHRISTMAS

Have yourself a merry little
 Christmas,
let you heart be light.
Next year all our troubles will be
 out of sight.
Have yourself a merry little
 Christmas,
make your Yuletide gay.
Next year all out troubles will be
 miles away.

Once again as in olden days, happy
 golden days of yore,
faithful friends who were dear to us
 will be near to us once more.

Someday soon we all will be
 together,
if the fates allow.
Until then, we'll have to muddle
 through somehow.
So have yourself a merry little
 Christmas now.

HERE COMES SANTA CLAUS
(Right Down Santa Claus Lane)

1. Here comes Santa Claus!
   Here comes Santa Claus!
   Right down Santa Claus Lane!

   Vixen and Blitzen and all his
      reindeer are pulling on the rein.
   Bells are ringing, children singing,
      all is merry and bright.
   Hang your stockings and say your
      pray'rs.
   'cause Santa Claus comes tonight.

2. Here comes Santa Claus!
   Here comes Santa Claus!
   Right down Santa Claus Lane!

   He's got a bag that is filled with
      toys for the boys and girls again.
   Hear those sleighbells jingle jangle,
      what a beautiful sight.
   Jump in bed, cover up your head,
   'cause Santa Claus comes tonight.

3. Here comes Santa Claus!
   Here comes Santa Claus!
   Right down Santa Claus Lane!

   He doesn't care if your rich or
      poor for he loves you just the
      same.
   Santa knows that we're God's
      children, that makes ev'rything
      right.
   Fill your hearts with a Christmas
      cheer,
   'cause Santa Claus comes tonight.

4. Here comes Santa Claus!
   Here comes Santa Claus!
   Right down Santa Claus Lane!

   He'll come around when the
      chimes ring out.
   then it's Christmas morn again.
   Peace on earth will come to all if
      we just follow the light.
   Let's give thanks to the Lord above,
   'cause Santa Claus comes tonight.

Words and Music by Gene Autry and
Oakley Haldeman
Copyright © 1947 (Renewed)
WESTERN MUSIC PUBLISHING CO.
International Copyright Secured
All Rights Reserved

A HOLLY JOLLY CHRISTMAS

Have a holly, jolly Christmas,
   it's the best time of the year.
I don't know if there'll be snow,
   but have a cup of cheer.

Have a holly, jolly Christmas,
   and when you walk down the
   street,
Say hello to friends you know,
   and ev'ryone you meet.

Oh, ho, the mistletoe, hung where
   you can see!
Somebody waits for you, kiss her
   once for me.

Have a holly, jolly Christmas,
   and in case you didn't hear.
Oh, by golly, have a holly, jolly
   Christmas this year.

Music and Lyrics by Johnny Marks
Copyright © 1962, 1964 (Renewed 1990, 1992)
St. Nicholas Music Inc.,
 1619 Broadway, New York, New York 10019
All Rights Reserved

I HEARD THE BELLS ON CHRISTMAS DAY

I heard the bells on Christmas Day,
   their old familiar carols play;
and wild and sweet the words repeat,
   of peace on earth, good will to men.

I thought as now this day had come,
   the belfries of all Christendom;
had rung so long the unbroken song,
   of peace on earth, good will to men.

And in despair, I bowed my head,
   "There is no peace on earth," I said:
"For hate is strong and mocks the song
   of peace on earth, good will to men."

Then pealed the bells more loud and
   deep, "God is not dead, nor doth
   He sleep;
the wrong shall fail, the right prevail
   with peace on earth, good will to
   men."

Words by Henry Longfellow
Adapted by Johnny Marks
Music by Johnny Marks
Copyright © 1956 (Renewed 1984)
St. Nicholas Music Inc.,
 1619 Broadway, New York, New York 10019
All Rights Reserved

JINGLE BELLS

1. Dashing through the snow, in a
      one horse open sleigh,
   o'er the fields we go, laughing all
      the way.
   Bells on bobtail ring, making
      spirits bright,
   what fun it is to ride and sing a
      sleighing song tonight!

   Jingle bells, jingle bells, jingle all
      the way.
   Oh, what fun it is to ride in a
      one horse open sleigh!
   Jingle bells, jingle bells, jingle all
      the way.
   Oh, what fun it is to ride in a
      one horse open sleigh!

2. A day or two ago I thought I'd take
      a ride,
   and soon Miss Fannie Bright was
      seated by my side.
   The horse was lean and lank,
      Miss fortune seemed his lot,
   he got into a drifted bank and
      we, we got upsot!

   Jingle bells, jingle bells, jingle all
      the way.
   Oh, what fun it is to ride in a
      one horse open sleigh!
   Jingle bells, jingle bells, jingle all
      the way.
   Oh, what fun it is to ride in a
      one horse open sleigh!

3. Now the ground is white, go it
      while you're young.
   Take the girls tonight and sing this
      sleighing song.
   Just get a bobtail bay, two-forty
      for his speed.
   then hitch him to an open sleigh
      and crack!
   you'll take the lead.

   Jingle bells, jingle bells, jingle all
      the way.
   Oh, what fun it is to ride in a
      one horse open sleigh!
   Jingle bells, jingle bells, jingle all
      the way.
   Oh, what fun it is to ride in a
      one horse open sleigh!

Words and Music by J. Pierpont
Copyright © 1995 by
HAL LEONARD CORPORATION
International Copyright Secured
All Rights Reserved

JINGLE-BELL ROCK

Jingle-bell, jingle-bell, jingle-bell rock,
  jingle-bell swing and jingle-bell ring.
Snowin' and blowin' up bushels of
  fun, now the jingle-hop has begun.

Jingle-bell, jingle-bell, jingle-bell rock,
  jingle-bells chime in jingle-bell time.
Dancin' and prancin' in Jingle-bell
  Square, in the frosty air.

What a bright time, it's the right
  time to rock the night away.
Jingle-bell time is a swell time,
  to go glidin' in a one horse sleigh.

Giddyap, jingle horse pick up your
  feet, jingle around the clock.
Mix and mingle in a jinglin' beat,
    that's the jingle-bell,
    that's the jingle-bell,
    that's the jingle-bell rock.

LET IT SNOW! LET IT SNOW! LET IT SNOW!

Oh, the weather outside is frightful,
  but the fire is so delightful;
and since we've no place to go,
  let it snow, let it snow, let it snow.

It doesn't show signs of stopping,
  and I brought some corn for
  popping;
the lights are turned way down low,
  let it snow, let it snow, let it snow.

When we finally kiss goodnight,
  how I'll hate going out in the
  storm.
But if you'll really hold me tight,
  all the way home I'll be warm.

The fire is slowly dying, and my
  dear, we're still good-byeing;
but as long as you love me so,
  let it snow, let it snow, let it snow.

O CHRISTMAS TREE

O Christmas tree, O Christmas tree,
  you stand in verdant beauty!
O Christmas tree, O Christmas tree,
  you stand in verdant beauty!

Your boughs are green in summer's
  glow, and do not fade in winter's
  snow.
O Christmas tree, O Christmas tree,
  you stand in verdant beauty!

O Christmas tree, O Christmas tree,
  much pleasure doth thou bring me!
O Christmas tree, O Christmas tree,
  much pleasure doth thou bring me!

For ev'ry year the Christmas tree,
  brings to us all both joy and glee.
O Christmas tree, O Christmas tree,
  much pleasure doth thou bring me!

O Christmas tree, O Christmas tree,
  thy candles shine out brightly!
O Christmas tree, O Christmas tree,
  thy candles shine out brightly!

Each bough doth hold its tiny light,
  that makes each toy to sparkle
  bright.
O Christmas tree, O Christmas tree,
  thy candles shine out brightly!

ROCKIN' AROUND THE CHRISTMAS TREE

Rockin' around the Christmas tree
  at the Christmas party hop.
Mistletoe hung where you can see
  ev'ry couple tries to stop.

Rockin' around the Christmas tree
  let the Christmas spirit ring.
Later we'll have some pumpkin pie
  and we'll do some caroling.

You will get a sentimental feeling
  when you hear,
voices singing, "Let's be jolly, deck
  the halls with boughs of holly."

Rockin' around the Christmas tree
  have a happy holiday.
Ev'ryone dancing merrily in the new
  old fashioned way.

RUDOLPH, THE RED-NOSED REINDEER

You know Dasher and Dancer and
  Prancer and Vixen,
Comet and Cupid and Donner and
  Blitzen,
but do you recall the most famous
  reindeer of all.

Rudolph, the red-nosed reindeer, had
  a very shiny nose.
And if you ever saw it, you would
  even say it glows.

All of the other reindeer, used to
  laugh and call him names.
They never let poor Rudolph join
  in any reindeer games.

Then one foggy Christmas Eve,
  Santa came to say,
"Rudolph, with your nose so bright
  won't you guide my sleigh
  tonight?"

Then how the reindeer loved him,
  as they shouted out with glee.
"Rudolph, the red-nosed reindeer,
  you'll go down in history!"

SANTA CLAUS IS COMIN' TO TOWN

You better watch out, you better not
  cry, better not pout, I'm telling
  you why:
Santa Claus is comin' to town.

He's making a list and checking it
  twice, gonna find out who's
  naughty and nice:
Santa Claus is comin' to town.

He sees you when you're sleepin',
  he knows when you're awake.
He knows if you've been bad or
  good, so be good for goodness
  sake.

Oh! You better watch out, you better
  not cry, better not pout, I'm telling
  you why:
Santa Claus is comin' to town.

Words by Haven Gillespie
Music by J. Fred Coots
© 1934 (Renewed 1962) EMI FEIST CATALOG INC.
Rights for the Extended Renewal Term in the
U.S. controlled by HAVEN GILLESPIE MUSIC and
EMI FEIST CATALOG INC.
All Rights outside the United States Controlled by
EMI FEIST CATALOG INC. (Publishing) and
WARNER BROS. PUBLICATIONS INC. (Print)
All Rights Reserved

SILVER BELLS

City sidewalks, busy sidewalks,
  dressed in holiday style.
In the air there's a feeling of
  Christmas.
Children laughing, people passing,
  meeting smile after smile,
and on ev'ry street corner you
  hear:

Silver bells, silver bells,
  it's Christmas time in the city.
Ring-a-ling, hear them ring,
  soon it will be Christmas day.

Strings of street lights, even stop-
  lights, blink a bright red and green.
As the shoppers rush home with
  their treasures.
Hear the snow crunch, see the kids
  bunch, this is Santa's big scene,
and above all this bustle you hear:

Silver bells, silver bells,
  it's Christmas time in the city.
Ring-a-ling, hear them ring,
  soon it will be Christmas day.

Words and Music by Jay Livingston and Ray Evans
Copyright © 1950 (Renewed 1977) by
Paramount Music Corporation
International Copyright Secured
All Rights Reserved

UP ON THE HOUSETOP

Up on the housetop reindeer pause,
  out jumps good old Santa Claus.
Down thro' the chimney with lots
  of toys.
all for the little ones, Christmas
  joys.

Ho, ho, ho! Who wouldn't go!
Ho, ho, ho! Who wouldn't go!
Up on the housetop click, click,
  click.
Down thro' the chimney with good
  Saint Nick.

First comes the stocking of little Nell,
  oh, dear Santa, fill it well.
Give her a dolly that laughs and
  cries, one that will open and shut
  her eyes.

Ho, ho, ho! Who wouldn't go!
Ho, ho, ho! Who wouldn't go!
Up on the housetop click, click,
  click.
Down thro' the chimney with good
  Saint Nick.

Traditional
Copyright © 1995 by
HAL LEONARD CORPORATION
International Copyright Secured
All Rights Reserved

WE WISH YOU A MERRY CHRISTMAS

We wish you a merry Christmas,
we wish you a merry Christmas,
we wish you a merry Christmas and
  a happy New Year!

Good tidings to you wherever you are.
Good tidings for Christmas and a
  happy New Year!

We wish you a merry Christmas,
we wish you a merry Christmas,
we wish you a merry Christmas and
  a happy New Year!

Traditional
Copyright © 1995 by
HAL LEONARD CORPORATION
International Copyright Secured
All Rights Reserved

JINGLE-BELL ROCK

Jingle-bell, jingle-bell, jingle-bell rock,
  jingle-bell swing and jingle-bell ring.
Snowin' and blówin' up bushels of
  fun, now the jingle-hop has begun.

Jingle-bell, jingle-bell, jingle-bell rock,
  jingle-bells chime in jingle-bell time.
Dancin' and prancin' in Jingle-bell
  Square, in the frosty air.

What a bright time, it's the right
  time to rock the night away.
Jingle-bell time is a swell time,
  to go glidin' in a one horse sleigh.

Giddyap, jingle horse pick up your
  feet, jingle around the clock.
Mix and mingle in a jinglin' beat,
  that's the jingle-bell,
  that's the jingle-bell,
  that's the jingle-bell rock.

LET IT SNOW! LET IT SNOW! LET IT SNOW!

Oh, the weather outside is frightful,
  but the fire is so delightful;
and since we've no place to go,
  let it snow, let it snow, let it snow.

It doesn't show signs of stopping,
  and I brought some corn for
  popping;
the lights are turned way down low,
  let it snow, let it snow, let it snow.

When we finally kiss goodnight,
  how I'll hate going out in the
  storm.
But if you'll really hold me tight,
  all the way home I'll be warm.

The fire is slowly dying, and my
  dear, we're still good-byeing;
but as long as you love me so,
  let it snow, let it snow, let it snow.

O CHRISTMAS TREE

O Christmas tree, O Christmas tree,
  you stand in verdant beauty!
O Christmas tree, O Christmas tree,
  you stand in verdant beauty!

Your boughs are green in summer's
  glow, and do not fade in winter's
  snow.
O Christmas tree, O Christmas tree,
  you stand in verdant beauty!

O Christmas tree, O Christmas tree,
  much pleasure doth thou bring me!
O Christmas tree, O Christmas tree,
  much pleasure doth thou bring me!

For ev'ry year the Christmas tree,
  brings to us all both joy and glee.
O Christmas tree, O Christmas tree,
  much pleasure doth thou bring me!

O Christmas tree, O Christmas tree,
  thy candles shine out brightly!
O Christmas tree, O Christmas tree,
  thy candles shine out brightly!

Each bough doth hold its tiny light,
  that makes each toy to sparkle
  bright.
O Christmas tree, O Christmas tree,
  thy candles shine out brightly!

ROCKIN' AROUND THE CHRISTMAS TREE

Rockin' around the Christmas tree
  at the Christmas party hop.
Mistletoe hung where you can see
  ev'ry couple tries to stop.

Rockin' around the Christmas tree
  let the Christmas spirit ring.
Later we'll have some pumpkin pie
  and we'll do some caroling.

You will get a sentimental feeling
  when you hear,
voices singing, "Let's be jolly, deck
  the halls with boughs of holly."

Rockin' around the Christmas tree
  have a happy holiday.
Ev'ryone dancing merrily in the new
  old fashioned way.

RUDOLPH, THE RED-NOSED REINDEER

You know Dasher and Dancer and
  Prancer and Vixen,
Comet and Cupid and Donner and
  Blitzen,
but do you recall the most famous
  reindeer of all.

Rudolph, the red-nosed reindeer, had
  a very shiny nose.
And if you ever saw it, you would
  even say it glows.

All of the other reindeer, used to
  laugh and call him names.
They never let poor Rudolph join
  in any reindeer games.

Then one foggy Christmas Eve,
  Santa came to say,
"Rudolph, with your nose so bright
  won't you guide my sleigh
  tonight?"

Then how the reindeer loved him,
  as they shouted out with glee.
"Rudolph, the red-nosed reindeer,
  you'll go down in history!"

SANTA CLAUS IS COMIN' TO TOWN

You better watch out, you better not
    cry, better not pout, I'm telling
    you why:
Santa Claus is comin' to town.

He's making a list and checking it
    twice, gonna find out who's
    naughty and nice:
Santa Claus is comin' to town.

He sees you when you're sleepin',
    he knows when you're awake.
He knows if you've been bad or
    good, so be good for goodness
    sake.

Oh! You better watch out, you better
    not cry, better not pout, I'm telling
    you why:
Santa Claus is comin' to town.

SILVER BELLS

City sidewalks, busy sidewalks,
    dressed in holiday style.
In the air there's a feeling of
    Christmas.
Children laughing, people passing,
    meeting smile after smile,
and on ev'ry street corner you
    hear:

Silver bells, silver bells,
    it's Christmas time in the city.
Ring-a-ling, hear them ring,
    soon it will be Christmas day.

Strings of street lights, even stop-
    lights, blink a bright red and green.
As the shoppers rush home with
    their treasures.
Hear the snow crunch, see the kids
    bunch, this is Santa's big scene,
and above all this bustle you hear:

Silver bells, silver bells,
    it's Christmas time in the city.
Ring-a-ling, hear them ring,
    soon it will be Christmas day.

UP ON THE HOUSETOP

Up on the housetop reindeer pause,
    out jumps good old Santa Claus.
Down thro' the chimney with lots
    of toys.
all for the little ones, Christmas
    joys.

Ho, ho, ho! Who wouldn't go!
Ho, ho, ho! Who wouldn't go!
Up on the housetop click, click,
    click.
Down thro' the chimney with good
    Saint Nick.

First comes the stocking of little Nell,
    oh, dear Santa, fill it well.
Give her a dolly that laughs and
    cries, one that will open and shut
    her eyes.

Ho, ho, ho! Who wouldn't go!
Ho, ho, ho! Who wouldn't go!
Up on the housetop click, click,
    click.
Down thro' the chimney with good
    Saint Nick.

WE WISH YOU A MERRY CHRISTMAS

We wish you a merry Christmas,
we wish you a merry Christmas,
we wish you a merry Christmas and
    a happy New Year!

Good tidings to you wherever you are.
Good tidings for Christmas and a
    happy New Year!

We wish you a merry Christmas,
we wish you a merry Christmas,
we wish you a merry Christmas and
    a happy New Year!

JINGLE-BELL ROCK

Jingle-bell, jingle-bell, jingle-bell rock,
  jingle-bell swing and jingle-bell ring.
Snowin' and blowin' up bushels of
  fun, now the jingle-hop has begun.

Jingle-bell, jingle-bell, jingle-bell rock,
  jingle-bells chime in jingle-bell time.
Dancin' and prancin' in Jingle-bell
  Square, in the frosty air.

What a bright time, it's the right
  time to rock the night away.
Jingle-bell time is a swell time,
  to go glidin' in a one horse sleigh.

Giddyap, jingle horse pick up your
  feet, jingle around the clock.
Mix and mingle in a jinglin' beat,
    that's the jingle-bell,
    that's the jingle-bell,
    that's the jingle-bell rock.

LET IT SNOW! LET IT SNOW! LET IT SNOW!

Oh, the weather outside is frightful,
  but the fire is so delightful;
and since we've no place to go,
  let it snow, let it snow, let it snow.

It doesn't show signs of stopping,
  and I brought some corn for
  popping;
the lights are turned way down low,
  let it snow, let it snow, let it snow.

When we finally kiss goodnight,
  how I'll hate going out in the
  storm.
But if you'll really hold me tight,
  all the way home I'll be warm.

The fire is slowly dying, and my
  dear, we're still good-byeing;
but as long as you love me so,
  let it snow, let it snow, let it snow.

O CHRISTMAS TREE

O Christmas tree, O Christmas tree,
  you stand in verdant beauty!
O Christmas tree, O Christmas tree,
  you stand in verdant beauty!

Your boughs are green in summer's
  glow, and do not fade in winter's
  snow.
O Christmas tree, O Christmas tree,
  you stand in verdant beauty!

O Christmas tree, O Christmas tree,
  much pleasure doth thou bring me!
O Christmas tree, O Christmas tree,
  much pleasure doth thou bring me!

For ev'ry year the Christmas tree,
  brings to us all both joy and glee.
O Christmas tree, O Christmas tree,
  much pleasure doth thou bring me!

O Christmas tree, O Christmas tree,
  thy candles shine out brightly!
O Christmas tree, O Christmas tree,
  thy candles shine out brightly!

Each bough doth hold its tiny light,
  that makes each toy to sparkle
  bright.
O Christmas tree, O Christmas tree,
  thy candles shine out brightly!

ROCKIN' AROUND THE CHRISTMAS TREE

Rockin' around the Christmas tree
  at the Christmas party hop.
Mistletoe hung where you can see
  ev'ry couple tries to stop.

Rockin' around the Christmas tree
  let the Christmas spirit ring.
Later we'll have some pumpkin pie
  and we'll do some caroling.

You will get a sentimental feeling
  when you hear,
voices singing, "Let's be jolly, deck
  the halls with boughs of holly."

Rockin' around the Christmas tree
  have a happy holiday.
Ev'ryone dancing merrily in the new
  old fashioned way.

RUDOLPH, THE RED-NOSED REINDEER

You know Dasher and Dancer and
  Prancer and Vixen,
Comet and Cupid and Donner and
  Blitzen,
but do you recall the most famous
  reindeer of all.

Rudolph, the red-nosed reindeer, had
  a very shiny nose.
And if you ever saw it, you would
  even say it glows.

All of the other reindeer, used to
  laugh and call him names.
They never let poor Rudolph join
  in any reindeer games.

Then one foggy Christmas Eve,
  Santa came to say,
"Rudolph, with your nose so bright
  won't you guide my sleigh
  tonight?"

Then how the reindeer loved him,
  as they shouted out with glee.
"Rudolph, the red-nosed reindeer,
  you'll go down in history!"

SANTA CLAUS IS COMIN' TO TOWN

You better watch out, you better not
    cry, better not pout, I'm telling
    you why:
Santa Claus is comin' to town.

He's making a list and checking it
    twice, gonna find out who's
    naughty and nice:
Santa Claus is comin' to town.

He sees you when you're sleepin',
    he knows when you're awake.
He knows if you've been bad or
    good, so be good for goodness
    sake.

Oh! You better watch out, you better
    not cry, better not pout, I'm telling
    you why:
Santa Claus is comin' to town.

SILVER BELLS

City sidewalks, busy sidewalks,
    dressed in holiday style.
In the air there's a feeling of
    Christmas.
Children laughing, people passing,
    meeting smile after smile,
and on ev'ry street corner you
    hear:

Silver bells, silver bells,
    it's Christmas time in the city.
Ring-a-ling, hear them ring,
    soon it will be Christmas day.

Strings of street lights, even stop-
    lights, blink a bright red and green.
As the shoppers rush home with
    their treasures.
Hear the snow crunch, see the kids
    bunch, this is Santa's big scene,
and above all this bustle you hear:

Silver bells, silver bells,
    it's Christmas time in the city.
Ring-a-ling, hear them ring,
    soon it will be Christmas day.

UP ON THE HOUSETOP

Up on the housetop reindeer pause,
    out jumps good old Santa Claus.
Down thro' the chimney with lots
    of toys.
all for the little ones, Christmas
    joys.

Ho, ho, ho! Who wouldn't go!
Ho, ho, ho! Who wouldn't go!
Up on the housetop click, click,
    click.
Down thro' the chimney with good
    Saint Nick.

First comes the stocking of little Nell,
    oh, dear Santa, fill it well.
Give her a dolly that laughs and
    cries, one that will open and shut
    her eyes.

Ho, ho, ho! Who wouldn't go!
Ho, ho, ho! Who wouldn't go!
Up on the housetop click, click,
    click.
Down thro' the chimney with good
    Saint Nick.

WE WISH YOU A MERRY CHRISTMAS

We wish you a merry Christmas,
we wish you a merry Christmas,
we wish you a merry Christmas and
    a happy New Year!

Good tidings to you wherever you are.
Good tidings for Christmas and a
    happy New Year!

We wish you a merry Christmas,
we wish you a merry Christmas,
we wish you a merry Christmas and
    a happy New Year!

JINGLE-BELL ROCK

Jingle-bell, jingle-bell, jingle-bell rock,
   jingle-bell swing and jingle-bell ring.
Snowin' and blówin' up bushels of
   fun, now the jingle-hop has begun.

Jingle-bell, jingle-bell, jingle-bell rock,
   jingle-bells chime in jingle-bell time.
Dancin' and prancin' in Jingle-bell
   Square, in the frosty air.

What a bright time, it's the right
   time to rock the night away.
Jingle-bell time is a swell time,
   to go glidin' in a one horse sleigh.

Giddyap, jingle horse pick up your
   feet, jingle around the clock.
Mix and mingle in a jinglin' beat,
   that's the jingle-bell,
   that's the jingle-bell,
   that's the jingle-bell rock.

LET IT SNOW! LET IT SNOW! LET IT SNOW!

Oh, the weather outside is frightful,
   but the fire is so delightful;
and since we've no place to go,
   let it snow, let it snow, let it snow.

It doesn't show signs of stopping,
   and I brought some corn for
   popping;
the lights are turned way down low,
   let it snow, let it snow, let it snow.

When we finally kiss goodnight,
   how I'll hate going out in the
   storm.
But if you'll really hold me tight,
   all the way home I'll be warm.

The fire is slowly dying, and my
   dear, we're still good-byeing;
but as long as you love me so,
   let it snow, let it snow, let it snow.

O CHRISTMAS TREE

O Christmas tree, O Christmas tree,
   you stand in verdant beauty!
O Christmas tree, O Christmas tree,
   you stand in verdant beauty!

Your boughs are green in summer's
   glow, and do not fade in winter's
   snow.
O Christmas tree, O Christmas tree,
   you stand in verdant beauty!

O Christmas tree, O Christmas tree,
   much pleasure doth thou bring me!
O Christmas tree, O Christmas tree,
   much pleasure doth thou bring me!

For ev'ry year the Christmas tree,
   brings to us all both joy and glee.
O Christmas tree, O Christmas tree,
   much pleasure doth thou bring me!

O Christmas tree, O Christmas tree,
   thy candles shine out brightly!
O Christmas tree, O Christmas tree,
   thy candles shine out brightly!

Each bough doth hold its tiny light,
   that makes each toy to sparkle
   bright.
O Christmas tree, O Christmas tree,
   thy candles shine out brightly!

ROCKIN' AROUND THE CHRISTMAS TREE

Rockin' around the Christmas tree
   at the Christmas party hop.
Mistletoe hung where you can see
   ev'ry couple tries to stop.

Rockin' around the Christmas tree
   let the Christmas spirit ring.
Later we'll have some pumpkin pie
   and we'll do some caroling.

You will get a sentimental feeling
   when you hear,
voices singing, "Let's be jolly, deck
   the halls with boughs of holly."

Rockin' around the Christmas tree
   have a happy holiday.
Ev'ryone dancing merrily in the new
   old fashioned way.

RUDOLPH, THE RED-NOSED REINDEER

You know Dasher and Dancer and
   Prancer and Vixen,
Comet and Cupid and Donner and
   Blitzen,
but do you recall the most famous
   reindeer of all.

Rudolph, the red-nosed reindeer, had
   a very shiny nose.
And if you ever saw it, you would
   even say it glows.

All of the other reindeer, used to
   laugh and call him names.
They never let poor Rudolph join
   in any reindeer games.

Then one foggy Christmas Eve,
   Santa came to say,
"Rudolph, with your nose so bright
   won't you guide my sleigh
   tonight?"

Then how the reindeer loved him,
   as they shouted out with glee.
"Rudolph, the red-nosed reindeer,
   you'll go down in history!"

SANTA CLAUS IS COMIN' TO TOWN

You better watch out, you better not
    cry, better not pout, I'm telling
    you why:
Santa Claus is comin' to town.

He's making a list and checking it
    twice, gonna find out who's
    naughty and nice:
Santa Claus is comin' to town.

He sees you when you're sleepin',
    he knows when you're awake.
He knows if you've been bad or
    good, so be good for goodness
    sake.

Oh! You better watch out, you better
    not cry, better not pout, I'm telling
    you why:
Santa Claus is comin' to town.

SILVER BELLS

City sidewalks, busy sidewalks,
    dressed in holiday style.
In the air there's a feeling of
    Christmas.
Children laughing, people passing,
    meeting smile after smile,
and on ev'ry street corner you
    hear:

Silver bells, silver bells,
    it's Christmas time in the city.
Ring-a-ling, hear them ring,
    soon it will be Christmas day.

Strings of street lights, even stop-
    lights, blink a bright red and green.
As the shoppers rush home with
    their treasures.
Hear the snow crunch, see the kids
    bunch, this is Santa's big scene,
and above all this bustle you hear:

Silver bells, silver bells,
    it's Christmas time in the city.
Ring-a-ling, hear them ring,
    soon it will be Christmas day.

UP ON THE HOUSETOP

Up on the housetop reindeer pause,
    out jumps good old Santa Claus.
Down thro' the chimney with lots
    of toys.
all for the little ones, Christmas
    joys.

Ho, ho, ho! Who wouldn't go!
Ho, ho, ho! Who wouldn't go!
Up on the housetop click, click,
    click.
Down thro' the chimney with good
    Saint Nick.

First comes the stocking of little Nell,
    oh, dear Santa, fill it well.
Give her a dolly that laughs and
    cries, one that will open and shut
    her eyes.

Ho, ho, ho! Who wouldn't go!
Ho, ho, ho! Who wouldn't go!
Up on the housetop click, click,
    click.
Down thro' the chimney with good
    Saint Nick.

WE WISH YOU A MERRY CHRISTMAS

We wish you a merry Christmas,
we wish you a merry Christmas,
we wish you a merry Christmas and
    a happy New Year!

Good tidings to you wherever you are.
Good tidings for Christmas and a
    happy New Year!

We wish you a merry Christmas,
we wish you a merry Christmas,
we wish you a merry Christmas and
    a happy New Year!

JINGLE-BELL ROCK

Jingle-bell, jingle-bell, jingle-bell rock,
  jingle-bell swing and jingle-bell ring.
Snowin' and blówin' up bushels of
  fun, now the jingle-hop has begun.

Jingle-bell, jingle-bell, jingle-bell rock,
  jingle-bells chime in jingle-bell time.
Dancin' and prancin' in Jingle-bell
  Square, in the frosty air.

What a bright time, it's the right
  time to rock the night away.
Jingle-bell time is a swell time,
  to go glidin' in a one horse sleigh.

Giddyap, jingle horse pick up your
  feet, jingle around the clock.
Mix and mingle in a jinglin' beat,
    that's the jingle-bell,
    that's the jingle-bell,
    that's the jingle-bell rock.

LET IT SNOW! LET IT SNOW! LET IT SNOW!

Oh, the weather outside is frightful,
  but the fire is so delightful;
and since we've no place to go,
  let it snow, let it snow, let it snow.

It doesn't show signs of stopping,
  and I brought some corn for
  popping;
the lights are turned way down low,
  let it snow, let it snow, let it snow.

When we finally kiss goodnight,
  how I'll hate going out in the
  storm.
But if you'll really hold me tight,
  all the way home I'll be warm.

The fire is slowly dying, and my
  dear, we're still good-byeing;
but as long as you love me so,
  let it snow, let it snow, let it snow.

O CHRISTMAS TREE

O Christmas tree, O Christmas tree,
  you stand in verdant beauty!
O Christmas tree, O Christmas tree,
  you stand in verdant beauty!

Your boughs are green in summer's
  glow, and do not fade in winter's
  snow.
O Christmas tree, O Christmas tree,
  you stand in verdant beauty!

O Christmas tree, O Christmas tree,
  much pleasure doth thou bring me!
O Christmas tree, O Christmas tree,
  much pleasure doth thou bring me!

For ev'ry year the Christmas tree,
  brings to us all both joy and glee.
O Christmas tree, O Christmas tree,
  much pleasure doth thou bring me!

O Christmas tree, O Christmas tree,
  thy candles shine out brightly!
O Christmas tree, O Christmas tree,
  thy candles shine out brightly!

Each bough doth hold its tiny light,
  that makes each toy to sparkle
  bright.
O Christmas tree, O Christmas tree,
  thy candles shine out brightly!

ROCKIN' AROUND THE CHRISTMAS TREE

Rockin' around the Christmas tree
  at the Christmas party hop.
Mistletoe hung where you can see
  ev'ry couple tries to stop.

Rockin' around the Christmas tree
  let the Christmas spirit ring.
Later we'll have some pumpkin pie
  and we'll do some caroling.

You will get a sentimental feeling
  when you hear,
voices singing, "Let's be jolly, deck
  the halls with boughs of holly."

Rockin' around the Christmas tree
  have a happy holiday.
Ev'ryone dancing merrily in the new
  old fashioned way.

RUDOLPH, THE RED-NOSED REINDEER

You know Dasher and Dancer and
  Prancer and Vixen,
Comet and Cupid and Donner and
  Blitzen,
but do you recall the most famous
  reindeer of all.

Rudolph, the red-nosed reindeer, had
  a very shiny nose.
And if you ever saw it, you would
  even say it glows.

All of the other reindeer, used to
  laugh and call him names.
They never let poor Rudolph join
  in any reindeer games.

Then one foggy Christmas Eve,
  Santa came to say,
"Rudolph, with your nose so bright
  won't you guide my sleigh
  tonight?"

Then how the reindeer loved him,
  as they shouted out with glee.
"Rudolph, the red-nosed reindeer,
  you'll go down in history!"

SANTA CLAUS IS COMIN' TO TOWN

You better watch out, you better not
    cry, better not pout, I'm telling
    you why:
Santa Claus is comin' to town.

He's making a list and checking it
    twice, gonna find out who's
    naughty and nice:
Santa Claus is comin' to town.

He sees you when you're sleepin',
    he knows when you're awake.
He knows if you've been bad or
    good, so be good for goodness
    sake.

Oh! You better watch out, you better
    not cry, better not pout, I'm telling
    you why:
Santa Claus is comin' to town.

SILVER BELLS

City sidewalks, busy sidewalks,
    dressed in holiday style.
In the air there's a feeling of
    Christmas.
Children laughing, people passing,
    meeting smile after smile,
and on ev'ry street corner you
    hear:

Silver bells, silver bells,
    it's Christmas time in the city.
Ring-a-ling, hear them ring,
    soon it will be Christmas day.

Strings of street lights, even stop-
    lights, blink a bright red and green.
As the shoppers rush home with
    their treasures.
Hear the snow crunch, see the kids
    bunch, this is Santa's big scene,
and above all this bustle you hear:

Silver bells, silver bells,
    it's Christmas time in the city.
Ring-a-ling, hear them ring,
    soon it will be Christmas day.

UP ON THE HOUSETOP

Up on the housetop reindeer pause,
    out jumps good old Santa Claus.
Down thro' the chimney with lots
    of toys.
all for the little ones, Christmas
    joys.

Ho, ho, ho! Who wouldn't go!
Ho, ho, ho! Who wouldn't go!
Up on the housetop click, click,
    click.
Down thro' the chimney with good
    Saint Nick.

First comes the stocking of little Nell,
    oh, dear Santa, fill it well.
Give her a dolly that laughs and
    cries, one that will open and shut
    her eyes.

Ho, ho, ho! Who wouldn't go!
Ho, ho, ho! Who wouldn't go!
Up on the housetop click, click,
    click.
Down thro' the chimney with good
    Saint Nick.

WE WISH YOU A MERRY CHRISTMAS

We wish you a merry Christmas,
we wish you a merry Christmas,
we wish you a merry Christmas and
    a happy New Year!

Good tidings to you wherever you are.
Good tidings for Christmas and a
    happy New Year!

We wish you a merry Christmas,
we wish you a merry Christmas,
we wish you a merry Christmas and
    a happy New Year!

JINGLE-BELL ROCK

Jingle-bell, jingle-bell, jingle-bell rock,
  jingle-bell swing and jingle-bell ring.
Snowin' and blówin' up bushels of
  fun, now the jingle-hop has begun.

Jingle-bell, jingle-bell, jingle-bell rock,
  jingle-bells chime in jingle-bell time.
Dancin' and prancin' in Jingle-bell
  Square, in the frosty air.

What a bright time, it's the right
  time to rock the night away.
Jingle-bell time is a swell time,
  to go glidin' in a one horse sleigh.

Giddyap, jingle horse pick up your
  feet, jingle around the clock.
Mix and mingle in a jinglin' beat,
  that's the jingle-bell,
  that's the jingle-bell,
  that's the jingle-bell rock.

LET IT SNOW! LET IT SNOW! LET IT SNOW!

Oh, the weather outside is frightful,
  but the fire is so delightful;
and since we've no place to go,
  let it snow, let it snow, let it snow.

It doesn't show signs of stopping,
  and I brought some corn for
  popping;
the lights are turned way down low,
  let it snow, let it snow, let it snow.

When we finally kiss goodnight,
  how I'll hate going out in the
  storm.
But if you'll really hold me tight,
  all the way home I'll be warm.

The fire is slowly dying, and my
  dear, we're still good-byeing;
but as long as you love me so,
  let it snow, let it snow, let it snow.

O CHRISTMAS TREE

O Christmas tree, O Christmas tree,
  you stand in verdant beauty!
O Christmas tree, O Christmas tree,
  you stand in verdant beauty!

Your boughs are green in summer's
  glow, and do not fade in winter's
  snow.
O Christmas tree, O Christmas tree,
  you stand in verdant beauty!

O Christmas tree, O Christmas tree,
  much pleasure doth thou bring me!
O Christmas tree, O Christmas tree,
  much pleasure doth thou bring me!

For ev'ry year the Christmas tree,
  brings to us all both joy and glee.
O Christmas tree, O Christmas tree,
  much pleasure doth thou bring me!

O Christmas tree, O Christmas tree,
  thy candles shine out brightly!
O Christmas tree, O Christmas tree,
  thy candles shine out brightly!

Each bough doth hold its tiny light,
  that makes each toy to sparkle
  bright.
O Christmas tree, O Christmas tree,
  thy candles shine out brightly!

ROCKIN' AROUND THE CHRISTMAS TREE

Rockin' around the Christmas tree
  at the Christmas party hop.
Mistletoe hung where you can see
  ev'ry couple tries to stop.

Rockin' around the Christmas tree
  let the Christmas spirit ring.
Later we'll have some pumpkin pie
  and we'll do some caroling.

You will get a sentimental feeling
  when you hear,
voices singing, "Let's be jolly, deck
  the halls with boughs of holly."

Rockin' around the Christmas tree
  have a happy holiday.
Ev'ryone dancing merrily in the new
  old fashioned way.

RUDOLPH, THE RED-NOSED REINDEER

You know Dasher and Dancer and
  Prancer and Vixen,
Comet and Cupid and Donner and
  Blitzen,
but do you recall the most famous
  reindeer of all.

Rudolph, the red-nosed reindeer, had
  a very shiny nose.
And if you ever saw it, you would
  even say it glows.

All of the other reindeer, used to
  laugh and call him names.
They never let poor Rudolph join
  in any reindeer games.

Then one foggy Christmas Eve,
  Santa came to say,
"Rudolph, with your nose so bright
  won't you guide my sleigh
  tonight?"

Then how the reindeer loved him,
  as they shouted out with glee.
"Rudolph, the red-nosed reindeer,
  you'll go down in history!"

SANTA CLAUS IS COMIN' TO TOWN

You better watch out, you better not
  cry, better not pout, I'm telling
  you why:
Santa Claus is comin' to town.

He's making a list and checking it
  twice, gonna find out who's
  naughty and nice:
Santa Claus is comin' to town.

He sees you when you're sleepin',
  he knows when you're awake.
He knows if you've been bad or
  good, so be good for goodness
  sake.

Oh! You better watch out, you better
  not cry, better not pout, I'm telling
  you why:
Santa Claus is comin' to town.

SILVER BELLS

City sidewalks, busy sidewalks,
  dressed in holiday style.
In the air there's a feeling of
  Christmas.
Children laughing, people passing,
  meeting smile after smile,
and on ev'ry street corner you
  hear:

Silver bells, silver bells,
  it's Christmas time in the city.
Ring-a-ling, hear them ring,
  soon it will be Christmas day.

Strings of street lights, even stop-
  lights, blink a bright red and green.
As the shoppers rush home with
  their treasures.
Hear the snow crunch, see the kids
  bunch, this is Santa's big scene,
and above all this bustle you hear:

Silver bells, silver bells,
  it's Christmas time in the city.
Ring-a-ling, hear them ring,
  soon it will be Christmas day.

UP ON THE HOUSETOP

Up on the housetop reindeer pause,
  out jumps good old Santa Claus.
Down thro' the chimney with lots
  of toys.
all for the little ones, Christmas
  joys.

Ho, ho, ho! Who wouldn't go!
Ho, ho, ho! Who wouldn't go!
Up on the housetop click, click,
  click.
Down thro' the chimney with good
  Saint Nick.

First comes the stocking of little Nell,
  oh, dear Santa, fill it well.
Give her a dolly that laughs and
  cries, one that will open and shut
  her eyes.

Ho, ho, ho! Who wouldn't go!
Ho, ho, ho! Who wouldn't go!
Up on the housetop click, click,
  click.
Down thro' the chimney with good
  Saint Nick.

WE WISH YOU A MERRY CHRISTMAS

We wish you a merry Christmas,
we wish you a merry Christmas,
we wish you a merry Christmas and
  a happy New Year!

Good tidings to you wherever you are.
Good tidings for Christmas and a
  happy New Year!

We wish you a merry Christmas,
we wish you a merry Christmas,
we wish you a merry Christmas and
  a happy New Year!

JINGLE-BELL ROCK

Jingle-bell, jingle-bell, jingle-bell rock,
    jingle-bell swing and jingle-bell ring.
Snowin' and blowin' up bushels of
    fun, now the jingle-hop has begun.

Jingle-bell, jingle-bell, jingle-bell rock,
    jingle-bells chime in jingle-bell time.
Dancin' and prancin' in Jingle-bell
    Square, in the frosty air.

What a bright time, it's the right
    time to rock the night away.
Jingle-bell time is a swell time,
    to go glidin' in a one horse sleigh.

Giddyap, jingle horse pick up your
    feet, jingle around the clock.
Mix and mingle in a jinglin' beat,
    that's the jingle-bell,
    that's the jingle-bell,
    that's the jingle-bell rock.

LET IT SNOW! LET IT SNOW! LET IT SNOW!

Oh, the weather outside is frightful,
    but the fire is so delightful;
and since we've no place to go,
    let it snow, let it snow, let it snow.

It doesn't show signs of stopping,
    and I brought some corn for
    popping;
the lights are turned way down low,
    let it snow, let it snow, let it snow.

When we finally kiss goodnight,
    how I'll hate going out in the
    storm.
But if you'll really hold me tight,
    all the way home I'll be warm.

The fire is slowly dying, and my
    dear, we're still good-byeing;
but as long as you love me so,
    let it snow, let it snow, let it snow.

O CHRISTMAS TREE

O Christmas tree, O Christmas tree,
    you stand in verdant beauty!
O Christmas tree, O Christmas tree,
    you stand in verdant beauty!

Your boughs are green in summer's
    glow, and do not fade in winter's
    snow.
O Christmas tree, O Christmas tree,
    you stand in verdant beauty!

O Christmas tree, O Christmas tree,
    much pleasure doth thou bring me!
O Christmas tree, O Christmas tree,
    much pleasure doth thou bring me!

For ev'ry year the Christmas tree,
    brings to us all both joy and glee.
O Christmas tree, O Christmas tree,
    much pleasure doth thou bring me!

O Christmas tree, O Christmas tree,
    thy candles shine out brightly!
O Christmas tree, O Christmas tree,
    thy candles shine out brightly!

Each bough doth hold its tiny light,
    that makes each toy to sparkle
    bright.
O Christmas tree, O Christmas tree,
    thy candles shine out brightly!

ROCKIN' AROUND THE CHRISTMAS TREE

Rockin' around the Christmas tree
    at the Christmas party hop.
Mistletoe hung where you can see
    ev'ry couple tries to stop.

Rockin' around the Christmas tree
    let the Christmas spirit ring.
Later we'll have some pumpkin pie
    and we'll do some caroling.

You will get a sentimental feeling
    when you hear,
voices singing, "Let's be jolly, deck
    the halls with boughs of holly."

Rockin' around the Christmas tree
    have a happy holiday.
Ev'ryone dancing merrily in the new
    old fashioned way.

RUDOLPH, THE RED-NOSED REINDEER

You know Dasher and Dancer and
    Prancer and Vixen,
Comet and Cupid and Donner and
    Blitzen,
but do you recall the most famous
    reindeer of all.

Rudolph, the red-nosed reindeer, had
    a very shiny nose.
And if you ever saw it, you would
    even say it glows.

All of the other reindeer, used to
    laugh and call him names.
They never let poor Rudolph join
    in any reindeer games.

Then one foggy Christmas Eve,
    Santa came to say,
"Rudolph, with your nose so bright
    won't you guide my sleigh
    tonight?"

Then how the reindeer loved him,
    as they shouted out with glee.
"Rudolph, the red-nosed reindeer,
    you'll go down in history!"

SANTA CLAUS IS COMIN' TO TOWN

You better watch out, you better not
  cry, better not pout, I'm telling
  you why:
Santa Claus is comin' to town.

He's making a list and checking it
  twice, gonna find out who's
  naughty and nice:
Santa Claus is comin' to town.

He sees you when you're sleepin',
  he knows when you're awake.
He knows if you've been bad or
  good, so be good for goodness
  sake.

Oh! You better watch out, you better
  not cry, better not pout, I'm telling
  you why:
Santa Claus is comin' to town.

SILVER BELLS

City sidewalks, busy sidewalks,
  dressed in holiday style.
In the air there's a feeling of
  Christmas.
Children laughing, people passing,
  meeting smile after smile,
and on ev'ry street corner you
  hear:

Silver bells, silver bells,
  it's Christmas time in the city.
Ring-a-ling, hear them ring,
  soon it will be Christmas day.

Strings of street lights, even stop-
  lights, blink a bright red and green.
As the shoppers rush home with
  their treasures.
Hear the snow crunch, see the kids
  bunch, this is Santa's big scene,
and above all this bustle you hear:

Silver bells, silver bells,
  it's Christmas time in the city.
Ring-a-ling, hear them ring,
  soon it will be Christmas day.

UP ON THE HOUSETOP

Up on the housetop reindeer pause,
  out jumps good old Santa Claus.
Down thro' the chimney with lots
  of toys.
all for the little ones, Christmas
  joys.

Ho, ho, ho! Who wouldn't go!
Ho, ho, ho! Who wouldn't go!
Up on the housetop click, click,
  click.
Down thro' the chimney with good
  Saint Nick.

First comes the stocking of little Nell,
  oh, dear Santa, fill it well.
Give her a dolly that laughs and
  cries, one that will open and shut
  her eyes.

Ho, ho, ho! Who wouldn't go!
Ho, ho, ho! Who wouldn't go!
Up on the housetop click, click,
  click.
Down thro' the chimney with good
  Saint Nick.

WE WISH YOU A MERRY CHRISTMAS

We wish you a merry Christmas,
we wish you a merry Christmas,
we wish you a merry Christmas and
  a happy New Year!

Good tidings to you wherever you are.
Good tidings for Christmas and a
  happy New Year!

We wish you a merry Christmas,
we wish you a merry Christmas,
we wish you a merry Christmas and
  a happy New Year!

JINGLE-BELL ROCK

Jingle-bell, jingle-bell, jingle-bell rock,
  jingle-bell swing and jingle-bell ring.
Snowin' and blówin' up bushels of
  fun, now the jingle-hop has begun.

Jingle-bell, jingle-bell, jingle-bell rock,
  jingle-bells chime in jingle-bell time.
Dancin' and prancin' in Jingle-bell
  Square, in the frosty air.

What a bright time, it's the right
  time to rock the night away.
Jingle-bell time is a swell time,
  to go glidin' in a one horse sleigh.

Giddyap, jingle horse pick up your
  feet, jingle around the clock.
Mix and mingle in a jinglin' beat,
  that's the jingle-bell,
  that's the jingle-bell,
  that's the jingle-bell rock.

LET IT SNOW! LET IT SNOW! LET IT SNOW!

Oh, the weather outside is frightful,
  but the fire is so delightful;
and since we've no place to go,
  let it snow, let it snow, let it snow.

It doesn't show signs of stopping,
  and I brought some corn for
  popping;
the lights are turned way down low,
  let it snow, let it snow, let it snow.

When we finally kiss goodnight,
  how I'll hate going out in the
  storm.
But if you'll really hold me tight,
  all the way home I'll be warm.

The fire is slowly dying, and my
  dear, we're still good-byeing;
but as long as you love me so,
  let it snow, let it snow, let it snow.

O CHRISTMAS TREE

O Christmas tree, O Christmas tree,
  you stand in verdant beauty!
O Christmas tree, O Christmas tree,
  you stand in verdant beauty!

Your boughs are green in summer's
  glow, and do not fade in winter's
  snow.
O Christmas tree, O Christmas tree,
  you stand in verdant beauty!

O Christmas tree, O Christmas tree,
  much pleasure doth thou bring me!
O Christmas tree, O Christmas tree,
  much pleasure doth thou bring me!

For ev'ry year the Christmas tree,
  brings to us all both joy and glee.
O Christmas tree, O Christmas tree,
  much pleasure doth thou bring me!

O Christmas tree, O Christmas tree,
  thy candles shine out brightly!
O Christmas tree, O Christmas tree,
  thy candles shine out brightly!

Each bough doth hold its tiny light,
  that makes each toy to sparkle
  bright.
O Christmas tree, O Christmas tree,
  thy candles shine out brightly!

ROCKIN' AROUND THE CHRISTMAS TREE

Rockin' around the Christmas tree
  at the Christmas party hop.
Mistletoe hung where you can see
  ev'ry couple tries to stop.

Rockin' around the Christmas tree
  let the Christmas spirit ring.
Later we'll have some pumpkin pie
  and we'll do some caroling.

You will get a sentimental feeling
  when you hear,
voices singing, "Let's be jolly, deck
  the halls with boughs of holly."

Rockin' around the Christmas tree
  have a happy holiday.
Ev'ryone dancing merrily in the new
  old fashioned way.

RUDOLPH, THE RED-NOSED REINDEER

You know Dasher and Dancer and
  Prancer and Vixen,
Comet and Cupid and Donner and
  Blitzen,
but do you recall the most famous
  reindeer of all.

Rudolph, the red-nosed reindeer, had
  a very shiny nose.
And if you ever saw it, you would
  even say it glows.

All of the other reindeer, used to
  laugh and call him names.
They never let poor Rudolph join
  in any reindeer games.

Then one foggy Christmas Eve,
  Santa came to say,
"Rudolph, with your nose so bright
  won't you guide my sleigh
  tonight?"

Then how the reindeer loved him,
  as they shouted out with glee.
"Rudolph, the red-nosed reindeer,
  you'll go down in history!"

SANTA CLAUS IS COMIN' TO TOWN

You better watch out, you better not
    cry, better not pout, I'm telling
    you why:
Santa Claus is comin' to town.

He's making a list and checking it
    twice, gonna find out who's
    naughty and nice:
Santa Claus is comin' to town.

He sees you when you're sleepin',
    he knows when you're awake.
He knows if you've been bad or
    good, so be good for goodness
    sake.

Oh! You better watch out, you better
    not cry, better not pout, I'm telling
    you why:
Santa Claus is comin' to town.

SILVER BELLS

City sidewalks, busy sidewalks,
    dressed in holiday style.
In the air there's a feeling of
    Christmas.
Children laughing, people passing,
    meeting smile after smile,
and on ev'ry street corner you
    hear:

Silver bells, silver bells,
    it's Christmas time in the city.
Ring-a-ling, hear them ring,
    soon it will be Christmas day.

Strings of street lights, even stop-
    lights, blink a bright red and green.
As the shoppers rush home with
    their treasures.
Hear the snow crunch, see the kids
    bunch, this is Santa's big scene,
and above all this bustle you hear:

Silver bells, silver bells,
    it's Christmas time in the city.
Ring-a-ling, hear them ring,
    soon it will be Christmas day.

UP ON THE HOUSETOP

Up on the housetop reindeer pause,
    out jumps good old Santa Claus.
Down thro' the chimney with lots
    of toys.
all for the little ones, Christmas
    joys.

Ho, ho, ho! Who wouldn't go!
Ho, ho, ho! Who wouldn't go!
Up on the housetop click, click,
    click.
Down thro' the chimney with good
    Saint Nick.

First comes the stocking of little Nell,
    oh, dear Santa, fill it well.
Give her a dolly that laughs and
    cries, one that will open and shut
    her eyes.

Ho, ho, ho! Who wouldn't go!
Ho, ho, ho! Who wouldn't go!
Up on the housetop click, click,
    click.
Down thro' the chimney with good
    Saint Nick.

WE WISH YOU A MERRY CHRISTMAS

We wish you a merry Christmas,
we wish you a merry Christmas,
we wish you a merry Christmas and
    a happy New Year!

Good tidings to you wherever you are.
Good tidings for Christmas and a
    happy New Year!

We wish you a merry Christmas,
we wish you a merry Christmas,
we wish you a merry Christmas and
    a happy New Year!

JINGLE-BELL ROCK

Jingle-bell, jingle-bell, jingle-bell rock,
    jingle-bell swing and jingle-bell ring.
Snowin' and bl6win' up bushels of
    fun, now the jingle-hop has begun.

Jingle-bell, jingle-bell, jingle-bell rock,
    jingle-bells chime in jingle-bell time.
Dancin' and prancin' in Jingle-bell
    Square, in the frosty air.

What a bright time, it's the right
    time to rock the night away.
Jingle-bell time is a swell time,
    to go glidin' in a one horse sleigh.

Giddyap, jingle horse pick up your
    feet, jingle around the clock.
Mix and mingle in a jinglin' beat,
    that's the jingle-bell,
    that's the jingle-bell,
    that's the jingle-bell rock.

LET IT SNOW! LET IT SNOW! LET IT SNOW!

Oh, the weather outside is frightful,
    but the fire is so delightful;
and since we've no place to go,
    let it snow, let it snow, let it snow.

It doesn't show signs of stopping,
    and I brought some corn for
    popping;
the lights are turned way down low,
    let it snow, let it snow, let it snow.

When we finally kiss goodnight,
    how I'll hate going out in the
    storm.
But if you'll really hold me tight,
    all the way home I'll be warm.

The fire is slowly dying, and my
    dear, we're still good-byeing;
but as long as you love me so,
    let it snow, let it snow, let it snow.

O CHRISTMAS TREE

O Christmas tree, O Christmas tree,
    you stand in verdant beauty!
O Christmas tree, O Christmas tree,
    you stand in verdant beauty!

Your boughs are green in summer's
    glow, and do not fade in winter's
    snow.
O Christmas tree, O Christmas tree,
    you stand in verdant beauty!

O Christmas tree, O Christmas tree,
    much pleasure doth thou bring me!
O Christmas tree, O Christmas tree,
    much pleasure doth thou bring me!

For ev'ry year the Christmas tree,
    brings to us all both joy and glee.
O Christmas tree, O Christmas tree,
    much pleasure doth thou bring me!

O Christmas tree, O Christmas tree,
    thy candles shine out brightly!
O Christmas tree, O Christmas tree,
    thy candles shine out brightly!

Each bough doth hold its tiny light,
    that makes each toy to sparkle
    bright.
O Christmas tree, O Christmas tree,
    thy candles shine out brightly!

ROCKIN' AROUND THE CHRISTMAS TREE

Rockin' around the Christmas tree
    at the Christmas party hop.
Mistletoe hung where you can see
    ev'ry couple tries to stop.

Rockin' around the Christmas tree
    let the Christmas spirit ring.
Later we'll have some pumpkin pie
    and we'll do some caroling.

You will get a sentimental feeling
    when you hear,
voices singing, "Let's be jolly, deck
    the halls with boughs of holly."

Rockin' around the Christmas tree
    have a happy holiday.
Ev'ryone dancing merrily in the new
    old fashioned way.

RUDOLPH, THE RED-NOSED REINDEER

You know Dasher and Dancer and
    Prancer and Vixen,
Comet and Cupid and Donner and
    Blitzen,
but do you recall the most famous
    reindeer of all.

Rudolph, the red-nosed reindeer, had
    a very shiny nose.
And if you ever saw it, you would
    even say it glows.

All of the other reindeer, used to
    laugh and call him names.
They never let poor Rudolph join
    in any reindeer games.

Then one foggy Christmas Eve,
    Santa came to say,
"Rudolph, with your nose so bright
    won't you guide my sleigh
    tonight?"

Then how the reindeer loved him,
    as they shouted out with glee.
"Rudolph, the red-nosed reindeer,
    you'll go down in history!"

SANTA CLAUS IS COMIN' TO TOWN

You better watch out, you better not
    cry, better not pout, I'm telling
    you why:
Santa Claus is comin' to town.

He's making a list and checking it
    twice, gonna find out who's
    naughty and nice:
Santa Claus is comin' to town.

He sees you when you're sleepin',
    he knows when you're awake.
He knows if you've been bad or
    good, so be good for goodness
    sake.

Oh! You better watch out, you better
    not cry, better not pout, I'm telling
    you why:
Santa Claus is comin' to town.

SILVER BELLS

City sidewalks, busy sidewalks,
    dressed in holiday style.
In the air there's a feeling of
    Christmas.
Children laughing, people passing,
    meeting smile after smile,
and on ev'ry street corner you
    hear:

Silver bells, silver bells,
    it's Christmas time in the city.
Ring-a-ling, hear them ring,
    soon it will be Christmas day.

Strings of street lights, even stop-
    lights, blink a bright red and green.
As the shoppers rush home with
    their treasures.
Hear the snow crunch, see the kids
    bunch, this is Santa's big scene,
and above all this bustle you hear:

Silver bells, silver bells,
    it's Christmas time in the city.
Ring-a-ling, hear them ring,
    soon it will be Christmas day.

UP ON THE HOUSETOP

Up on the housetop reindeer pause,
    out jumps good old Santa Claus.
Down thro' the chimney with lots
    of toys.
all for the little ones, Christmas
    joys.

Ho, ho, ho! Who wouldn't go!
Ho, ho, ho! Who wouldn't go!
Up on the housetop click, click,
    click.
Down thro' the chimney with good
    Saint Nick.

First comes the stocking of little Nell,
    oh, dear Santa, fill it well.
Give her a dolly that laughs and
    cries, one that will open and shut
    her eyes.

Ho, ho, ho! Who wouldn't go!
Ho, ho, ho! Who wouldn't go!
Up on the housetop click, click,
    click.
Down thro' the chimney with good
    Saint Nick.

WE WISH YOU A MERRY CHRISTMAS

We wish you a merry Christmas,
we wish you a merry Christmas,
we wish you a merry Christmas and
    a happy New Year!

Good tidings to you wherever you are.
Good tidings for Christmas and a
    happy New Year!

We wish you a merry Christmas,
we wish you a merry Christmas,
we wish you a merry Christmas and
    a happy New Year!

JINGLE-BELL ROCK

Jingle-bell, jingle-bell, jingle-bell rock,
   jingle-bell swing and jingle-bell ring.
Snowin' and blówin' up bushels of
   fun, now the jingle-hop has begun.

Jingle-bell, jingle-bell, jingle-bell rock,
   jingle-bells chime in jingle-bell time.
Dancin' and prancin' in Jingle-bell
   Square, in the frosty air.

What a bright time, it's the right
   time to rock the night away.
Jingle-bell time is a swell time,
   to go glidin' in a one horse sleigh.

Giddyap, jingle horse pick up your
   feet, jingle around the clock.
Mix and mingle in a jinglin' beat,
   that's the jingle-bell,
   that's the jingle-bell,
   that's the jingle-bell rock.

LET IT SNOW! LET IT SNOW! LET IT SNOW!

Oh, the weather outside is frightful,
   but the fire is so delightful;
and since we've no place to go,
   let it snow, let it snow, let it snow.

It doesn't show signs of stopping,
   and I brought some corn for
   popping;
the lights are turned way down low,
   let it snow, let it snow, let it snow.

When we finally kiss goodnight,
   how I'll hate going out in the
   storm.
But if you'll really hold me tight,
   all the way home I'll be warm.

The fire is slowly dying, and my
   dear, we're still good-byeing;
but as long as you love me so,
   let it snow, let it snow, let it snow.

O CHRISTMAS TREE

O Christmas tree, O Christmas tree,
   you stand in verdant beauty!
O Christmas tree, O Christmas tree,
   you stand in verdant beauty!

Your boughs are green in summer's
   glow, and do not fade in winter's
   snow.
O Christmas tree, O Christmas tree,
   you stand in verdant beauty!

O Christmas tree, O Christmas tree,
   much pleasure doth thou bring me!
O Christmas tree, O Christmas tree,
   much pleasure doth thou bring me!

For ev'ry year the Christmas tree,
   brings to us all both joy and glee.
O Christmas tree, O Christmas tree,
   much pleasure doth thou bring me!

O Christmas tree, O Christmas tree,
   thy candles shine out brightly!
O Christmas tree, O Christmas tree,
   thy candles shine out brightly!

Each bough doth hold its tiny light,
   that makes each toy to sparkle
   bright.
O Christmas tree, O Christmas tree,
   thy candles shine out brightly!

ROCKIN' AROUND THE CHRISTMAS TREE

Rockin' around the Christmas tree
   at the Christmas party hop.
Mistletoe hung where you can see
   ev'ry couple tries to stop.

Rockin' around the Christmas tree
   let the Christmas spirit ring.
Later we'll have some pumpkin pie
   and we'll do some caroling.

You will get a sentimental feeling
   when you hear,
voices singing, "Let's be jolly, deck
   the halls with boughs of holly."

Rockin' around the Christmas tree
   have a happy holiday.
Ev'ryone dancing merrily in the new
   old fashioned way.

RUDOLPH, THE RED-NOSED REINDEER

You know Dasher and Dancer and
   Prancer and Vixen,
Comet and Cupid and Donner and
   Blitzen,
but do you recall the most famous
   reindeer of all.

Rudolph, the red-nosed reindeer, had
   a very shiny nose.
And if you ever saw it, you would
   even say it glows.

All of the other reindeer, used to
   laugh and call him names.
They never let poor Rudolph join
   in any reindeer games.

Then one foggy Christmas Eve,
   Santa came to say,
"Rudolph, with your nose so bright
   won't you guide my sleigh
   tonight?"

Then how the reindeer loved him,
   as they shouted out with glee.
"Rudolph, the red-nosed reindeer,
   you'll go down in history!"

SANTA CLAUS IS COMIN' TO TOWN

You better watch out, you better not
  cry, better not pout, I'm telling
  you why:
Santa Claus is comin' to town.

He's making a list and checking it
  twice, gonna find out who's
  naughty and nice:
Santa Claus is comin' to town.

He sees you when you're sleepin',
  he knows when you're awake.
He knows if you've been bad or
  good, so be good for goodness
  sake.

Oh! You better watch out, you better
  not cry, better not pout, I'm telling
  you why:
Santa Claus is comin' to town.

SILVER BELLS

City sidewalks, busy sidewalks,
  dressed in holiday style.
In the air there's a feeling of
  Christmas.
Children laughing, people passing,
  meeting smile after smile,
and on ev'ry street corner you
  hear:

Silver bells, silver bells,
  it's Christmas time in the city.
Ring-a-ling, hear them ring,
  soon it will be Christmas day.

Strings of street lights, even stop-
  lights, blink a bright red and green.
As the shoppers rush home with
  their treasures.
Hear the snow crunch, see the kids
  bunch, this is Santa's big scene,
and above all this bustle you hear:

Silver bells, silver bells,
  it's Christmas time in the city.
Ring-a-ling, hear them ring,
  soon it will be Christmas day.

UP ON THE HOUSETOP

Up on the housetop reindeer pause,
  out jumps good old Santa Claus.
Down thro' the chimney with lots
  of toys.
all for the little ones, Christmas
  joys.

Ho, ho, ho! Who wouldn't go!
Ho, ho, ho! Who wouldn't go!
Up on the housetop click, click,
  click.
Down thro' the chimney with good
  Saint Nick.

First comes the stocking of little Nell,
  oh, dear Santa, fill it well.
Give her a dolly that laughs and
  cries, one that will open and shut
  her eyes.

Ho, ho, ho! Who wouldn't go!
Ho, ho, ho! Who wouldn't go!
Up on the housetop click, click,
  click.
Down thro' the chimney with good
  Saint Nick.

WE WISH YOU A MERRY CHRISTMAS

We wish you a merry Christmas,
we wish you a merry Christmas,
we wish you a merry Christmas and
  a happy New Year!

Good tidings to you wherever you are.
Good tidings for Christmas and a
  happy New Year!

We wish you a merry Christmas,
we wish you a merry Christmas,
we wish you a merry Christmas and
  a happy New Year!

JINGLE-BELL ROCK

Jingle-bell, jingle-bell, jingle-bell rock,
   jingle-bell swing and jingle-bell ring.
Snowin' and blówin' up bushels of
   fun, now the jingle-hop has begun.

Jingle-bell, jingle-bell, jingle-bell rock,
   jingle-bells chime in jingle-bell time.
Dancin' and prancin' in Jingle-bell
   Square, in the frosty air.

What a bright time, it's the right
   time to rock the night away.
Jingle-bell time is a swell time,
   to go glidin' in a one horse sleigh.

Giddyap, jingle horse pick up your
   feet, jingle around the clock.
Mix and mingle in a jinglin' beat,
   that's the jingle-bell,
   that's the jingle-bell,
   that's the jingle-bell rock.

LET IT SNOW! LET IT SNOW! LET IT SNOW!

Oh, the weather outside is frightful,
   but the fire is so delightful;
and since we've no place to go,
   let it snow, let it snow, let it snow.

It doesn't show signs of stopping,
   and I brought some corn for
   popping;
the lights are turned way down low,
   let it snow, let it snow, let it snow.

When we finally kiss goodnight,
   how I'll hate going out in the
   storm.
But if you'll really hold me tight,
   all the way home I'll be warm.

The fire is slowly dying, and my
   dear, we're still good-byeing;
but as long as you love me so,
   let it snow, let it snow, let it snow.

O CHRISTMAS TREE

O Christmas tree, O Christmas tree,
   you stand in verdant beauty!
O Christmas tree, O Christmas tree,
   you stand in verdant beauty!

Your boughs are green in summer's
   glow, and do not fade in winter's
   snow.
O Christmas tree, O Christmas tree,
   you stand in verdant beauty!

O Christmas tree, O Christmas tree,
   much pleasure doth thou bring me!
O Christmas tree, O Christmas tree,
   much pleasure doth thou bring me!

For ev'ry year the Christmas tree,
   brings to us all both joy and glee.
O Christmas tree, O Christmas tree,
   much pleasure doth thou bring me!

O Christmas tree, O Christmas tree,
   thy candles shine out brightly!
O Christmas tree, O Christmas tree,
   thy candles shine out brightly!

Each bough doth hold its tiny light,
   that makes each toy to sparkle
   bright.
O Christmas tree, O Christmas tree,
   thy candles shine out brightly!

ROCKIN' AROUND THE CHRISTMAS TREE

Rockin' around the Christmas tree
   at the Christmas party hop.
Mistletoe hung where you can see
   ev'ry couple tries to stop.

Rockin' around the Christmas tree
   let the Christmas spirit ring.
Later we'll have some pumpkin pie
   and we'll do some caroling.

You will get a sentimental feeling
   when you hear,
voices singing, "Let's be jolly, deck
   the halls with boughs of holly."

Rockin' around the Christmas tree
   have a happy holiday.
Ev'ryone dancing merrily in the new
   old fashioned way.

RUDOLPH, THE RED-NOSED REINDEER

You know Dasher and Dancer and
   Prancer and Vixen,
Comet and Cupid and Donner and
   Blitzen,
but do you recall the most famous
   reindeer of all.

Rudolph, the red-nosed reindeer, had
   a very shiny nose.
And if you ever saw it, you would
   even say it glows.

All of the other reindeer, used to
   laugh and call him names.
They never let poor Rudolph join
   in any reindeer games.

Then one foggy Christmas Eve,
   Santa came to say,
"Rudolph, with your nose so bright
   won't you guide my sleigh
   tonight?"

Then how the reindeer loved him,
   as they shouted out with glee.
"Rudolph, the red-nosed reindeer,
   you'll go down in history!"

SANTA CLAUS IS COMIN' TO TOWN

You better watch out, you better not
  cry, better not pout, I'm telling
  you why:
Santa Claus is comin' to town.

He's making a list and checking it
  twice, gonna find out who's
  naughty and nice:
Santa Claus is comin' to town.

He sees you when you're sleepin',
  he knows when you're awake.
He knows if you've been bad or
  good, so be good for goodness
  sake.

Oh! You better watch out, you better
  not cry, better not pout, I'm telling
  you why:
Santa Claus is comin' to town.

SILVER BELLS

City sidewalks, busy sidewalks,
  dressed in holiday style.
In the air there's a feeling of
  Christmas.
Children laughing, people passing,
  meeting smile after smile,
and on ev'ry street corner you
  hear:

Silver bells, silver bells,
  it's Christmas time in the city.
Ring-a-ling, hear them ring,
  soon it will be Christmas day.

Strings of street lights, even stop-
  lights, blink a bright red and green.
As the shoppers rush home with
  their treasures.
Hear the snow crunch, see the kids
  bunch, this is Santa's big scene,
and above all this bustle you hear:

Silver bells, silver bells,
  it's Christmas time in the city.
Ring-a-ling, hear them ring,
  soon it will be Christmas day.

UP ON THE HOUSETOP

Up on the housetop reindeer pause,
  out jumps good old Santa Claus.
Down thro' the chimney with lots
  of toys.
all for the little ones, Christmas
  joys.

Ho, ho, ho! Who wouldn't go!
Ho, ho, ho! Who wouldn't go!
Up on the housetop click, click,
  click.
Down thro' the chimney with good
  Saint Nick.

First comes the stocking of little Nell,
  oh, dear Santa, fill it well.
Give her a dolly that laughs and
  cries, one that will open and shut
  her eyes.

Ho, ho, ho! Who wouldn't go!
Ho, ho, ho! Who wouldn't go!
Up on the housetop click, click,
  click.
Down thro' the chimney with good
  Saint Nick.

WE WISH YOU A MERRY CHRISTMAS

We wish you a merry Christmas,
we wish you a merry Christmas,
we wish you a merry Christmas and
  a happy New Year!

Good tidings to you wherever you are.
Good tidings for Christmas and a
  happy New Year!

We wish you a merry Christmas,
we wish you a merry Christmas,
we wish you a merry Christmas and
  a happy New Year!

JINGLE-BELL ROCK

Jingle-bell, jingle-bell, jingle-bell rock,
   jingle-bell swing and jingle-bell ring.
Snowin' and blowin' up bushels of
   fun, now the jingle-hop has begun.

Jingle-bell, jingle-bell, jingle-bell rock,
   jingle-bells chime in jingle-bell time.
Dancin' and prancin' in Jingle-bell
   Square, in the frosty air.

What a bright time, it's the right
   time to rock the night away.
Jingle-bell time is a swell time,
   to go glidin' in a one horse sleigh.

Giddyap, jingle horse pick up your
   feet, jingle around the clock.
Mix and mingle in a jinglin' beat,
   that's the jingle-bell,
   that's the jingle-bell,
   that's the jingle-bell rock.

LET IT SNOW! LET IT SNOW! LET IT SNOW!

Oh, the weather outside is frightful,
   but the fire is so delightful;
and since we've no place to go,
   let it snow, let it snow, let it snow.

It doesn't show signs of stopping,
   and I brought some corn for
   popping;
the lights are turned way down low,
   let it snow, let it snow, let it snow.

When we finally kiss goodnight,
   how I'll hate going out in the
   storm.
But if you'll really hold me tight,
   all the way home I'll be warm.

The fire is slowly dying, and my
   dear, we're still good-byeing;
but as long as you love me so,
   let it snow, let it snow, let it snow.

O CHRISTMAS TREE

O Christmas tree, O Christmas tree,
   you stand in verdant beauty!
O Christmas tree, O Christmas tree,
   you stand in verdant beauty!

Your boughs are green in summer's
   glow, and do not fade in winter's
   snow.
O Christmas tree, O Christmas tree,
   you stand in verdant beauty!

O Christmas tree, O Christmas tree,
   much pleasure doth thou bring me!
O Christmas tree, O Christmas tree,
   much pleasure doth thou bring me!

For ev'ry year the Christmas tree,
   brings to us all both joy and glee.
O Christmas tree, O Christmas tree,
   much pleasure doth thou bring me!

O Christmas tree, O Christmas tree,
   thy candles shine out brightly!
O Christmas tree, O Christmas tree,
   thy candles shine out brightly!

Each bough doth hold its tiny light,
   that makes each toy to sparkle
   bright.
O Christmas tree, O Christmas tree,
   thy candles shine out brightly!

ROCKIN' AROUND THE CHRISTMAS TREE

Rockin' around the Christmas tree
   at the Christmas party hop.
Mistletoe hung where you can see
   ev'ry couple tries to stop.

Rockin' around the Christmas tree
   let the Christmas spirit ring.
Later we'll have some pumpkin pie
   and we'll do some caroling.

You will get a sentimental feeling
   when you hear,
voices singing, "Let's be jolly, deck
   the halls with boughs of holly."

Rockin' around the Christmas tree
   have a happy holiday.
Ev'ryone dancing merrily in the new
   old fashioned way.

RUDOLPH, THE RED-NOSED REINDEER

You know Dasher and Dancer and
   Prancer and Vixen,
Comet and Cupid and Donner and
   Blitzen,
but do you recall the most famous
   reindeer of all.

Rudolph, the red-nosed reindeer, had
   a very shiny nose.
And if you ever saw it, you would
   even say it glows.

All of the other reindeer, used to
   laugh and call him names.
They never let poor Rudolph join
   in any reindeer games.

Then one foggy Christmas Eve,
   Santa came to say,
"Rudolph, with your nose so bright
   won't you guide my sleigh
   tonight?"

Then how the reindeer loved him,
   as they shouted out with glee.
"Rudolph, the red-nosed reindeer,
   you'll go down in history!"

SANTA CLAUS IS COMIN' TO TOWN

You better watch out, you better not
    cry, better not pout, I'm telling
    you why:
Santa Claus is comin' to town.

He's making a list and checking it
    twice, gonna find out who's
    naughty and nice:
Santa Claus is comin' to town.

He sees you when you're sleepin',
    he knows when you're awake.
He knows if you've been bad or
    good, so be good for goodness
    sake.

Oh! You better watch out, you better
    not cry, better not pout, I'm telling
    you why:
Santa Claus is comin' to town.

SILVER BELLS

City sidewalks, busy sidewalks,
    dressed in holiday style.
In the air there's a feeling of
    Christmas.
Children laughing, people passing,
    meeting smile after smile,
and on ev'ry street corner you
    hear:

Silver bells, silver bells,
    it's Christmas time in the city.
Ring-a-ling, hear them ring,
    soon it will be Christmas day.

Strings of street lights, even stop-
    lights, blink a bright red and green.
As the shoppers rush home with
    their treasures.
Hear the snow crunch, see the kids
    bunch, this is Santa's big scene,
and above all this bustle you hear:

Silver bells, silver bells,
    it's Christmas time in the city.
Ring-a-ling, hear them ring,
    soon it will be Christmas day.

UP ON THE HOUSETOP

Up on the housetop reindeer pause,
    out jumps good old Santa Claus.
Down thro' the chimney with lots
    of toys.
all for the little ones, Christmas
    joys.

Ho, ho, ho! Who wouldn't go!
Ho, ho, ho! Who wouldn't go!
Up on the housetop click, click,
    click.
Down thro' the chimney with good
    Saint Nick.

First comes the stocking of little Nell,
    oh, dear Santa, fill it well.
Give her a dolly that laughs and
    cries, one that will open and shut
    her eyes.

Ho, ho, ho! Who wouldn't go!
Ho, ho, ho! Who wouldn't go!
Up on the housetop click, click,
    click.
Down thro' the chimney with good
    Saint Nick.

WE WISH YOU A MERRY CHRISTMAS

We wish you a merry Christmas,
we wish you a merry Christmas,
we wish you a merry Christmas and
    a happy New Year!

Good tidings to you wherever you are.
Good tidings for Christmas and a
    happy New Year!

We wish you a merry Christmas,
we wish you a merry Christmas,
we wish you a merry Christmas and
    a happy New Year!

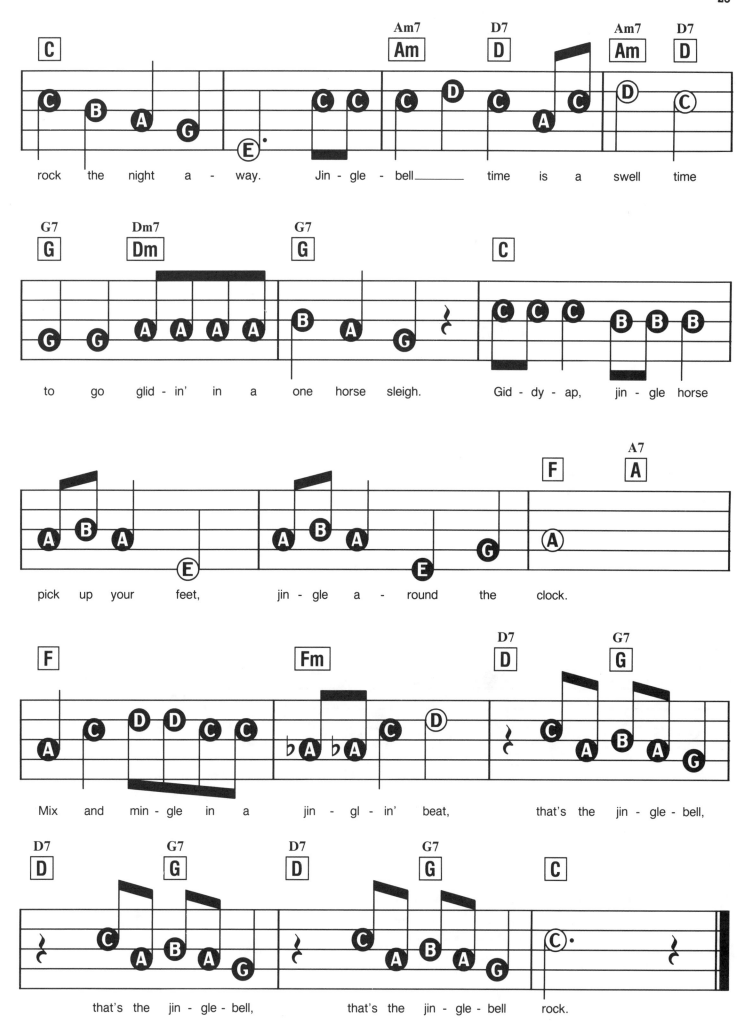

Jingle Bells

Registration 5
Rhythm: Fox Trot or Swing

Words and Music by
J. Pierpont

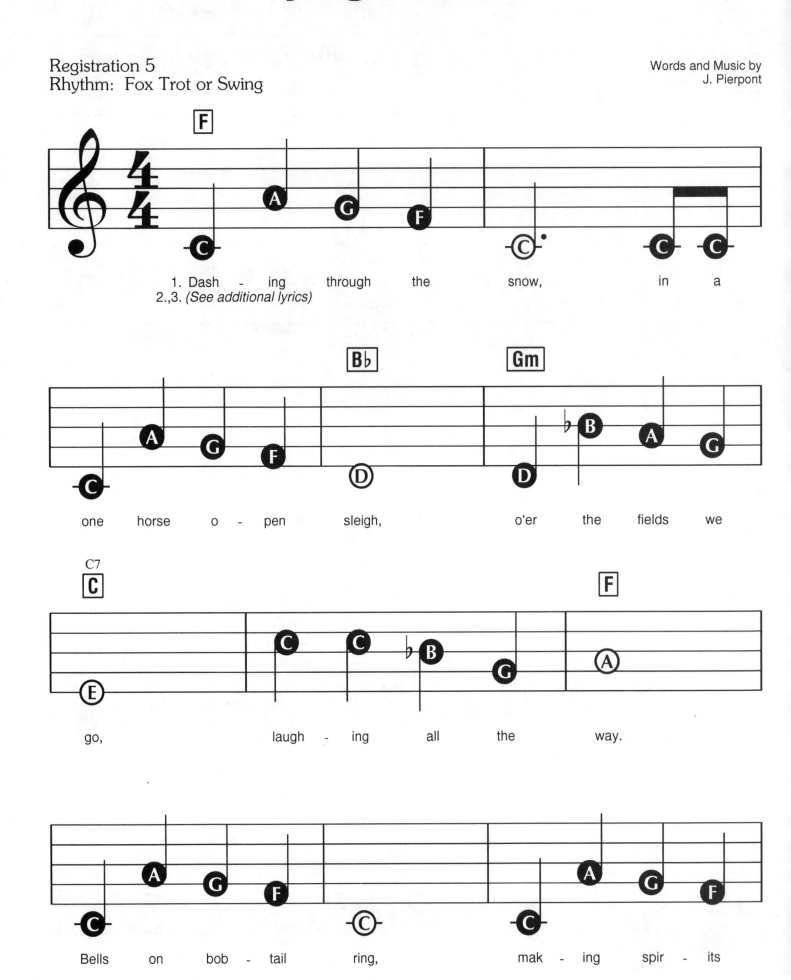

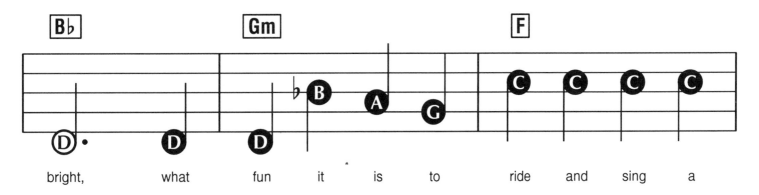

bright,   what   fun it is to ride and sing a

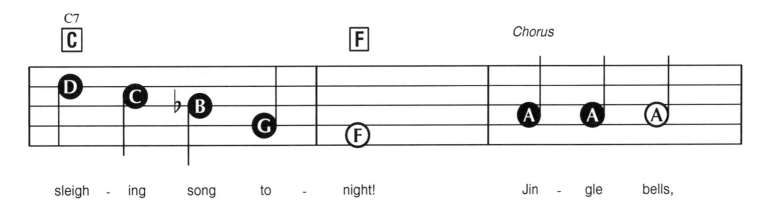

sleigh - ing   song to - night!   Jin - gle   bells,

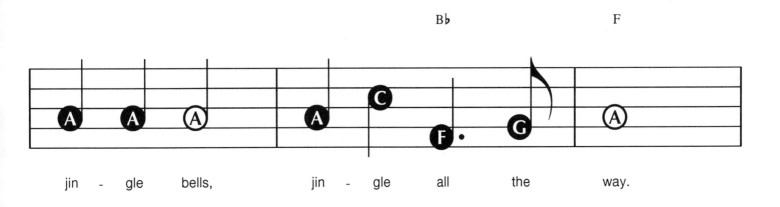

jin - gle bells,   jin - gle all the way.

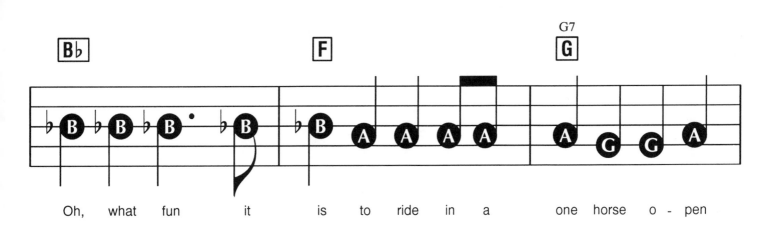

Oh, what fun it is to ride in a   one horse o - pen

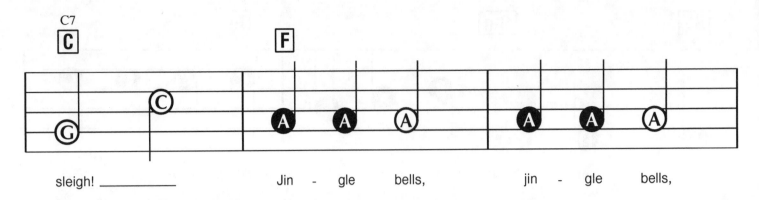

sleigh! _____   Jin - gle   bells,   jin - gle   bells,

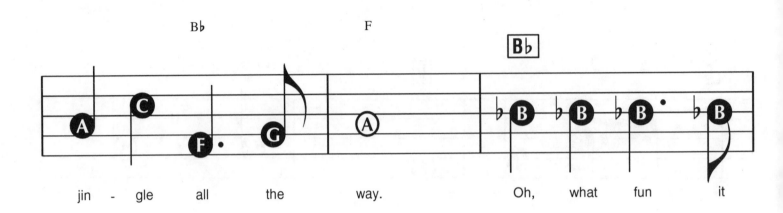

jin - gle   all   the   way.   Oh,   what   fun   it

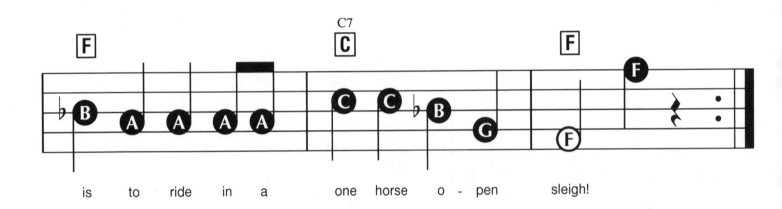

is   to   ride   in   a   one   horse   o - pen   sleigh!

Additional Lyrics

2. A day or two ago I thought I'd
   take a ride,
and soon Miss Fannie Bright was
   seated by my side.
The horse was lean and lank,
   Miss Fortune seemed his lot,
he got into a drifted bank and we,
   we got upsot!

Chorus

3. Now the ground is white,
   go it while you're young.
Take the girls tonight and sing this
   sleighing song.
Just get a bobtail bay, two-forty
   for his speed,
then hitch him to an open sleigh and
   crack! you'll take the lead.

Chorus

O Christmas Tree

Registration 3

Traditional

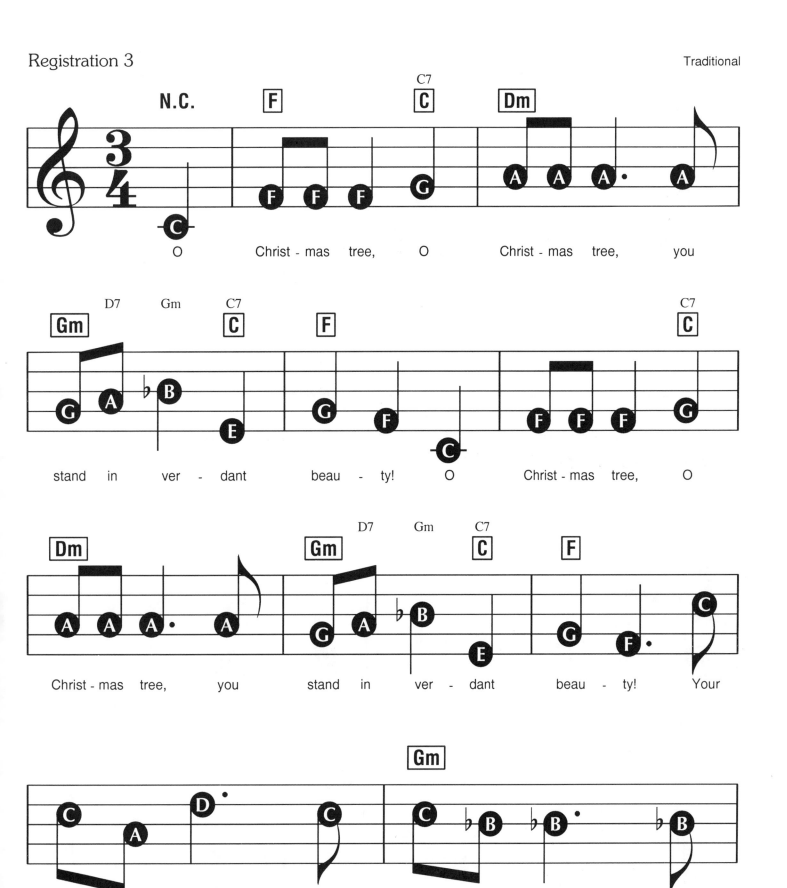

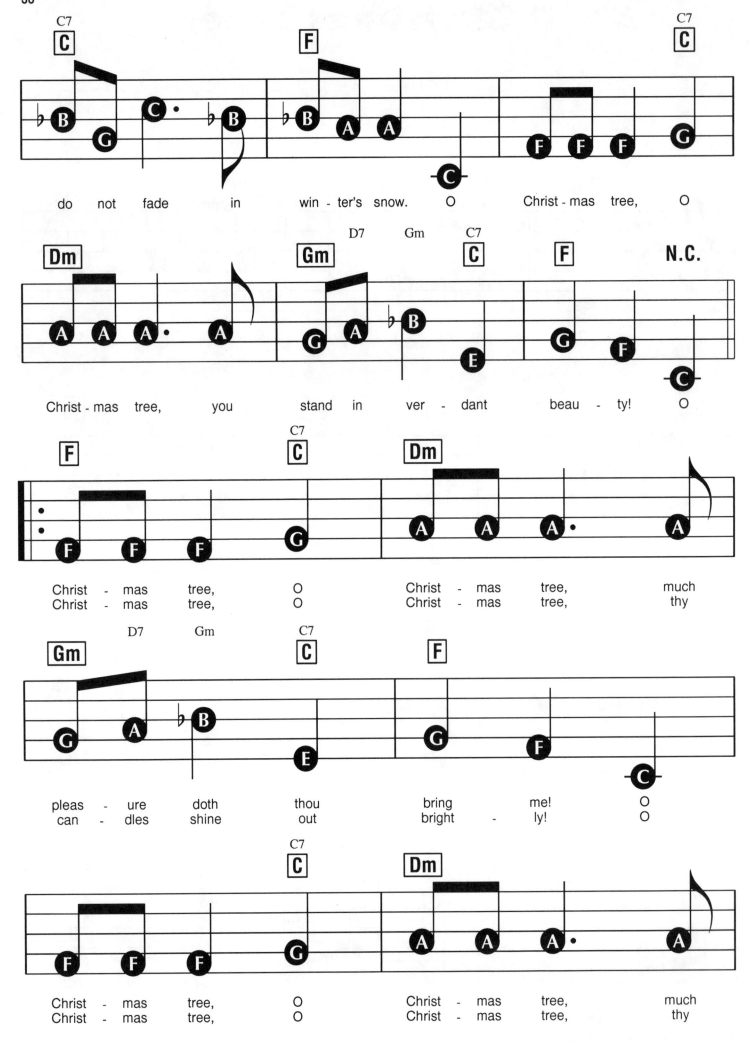

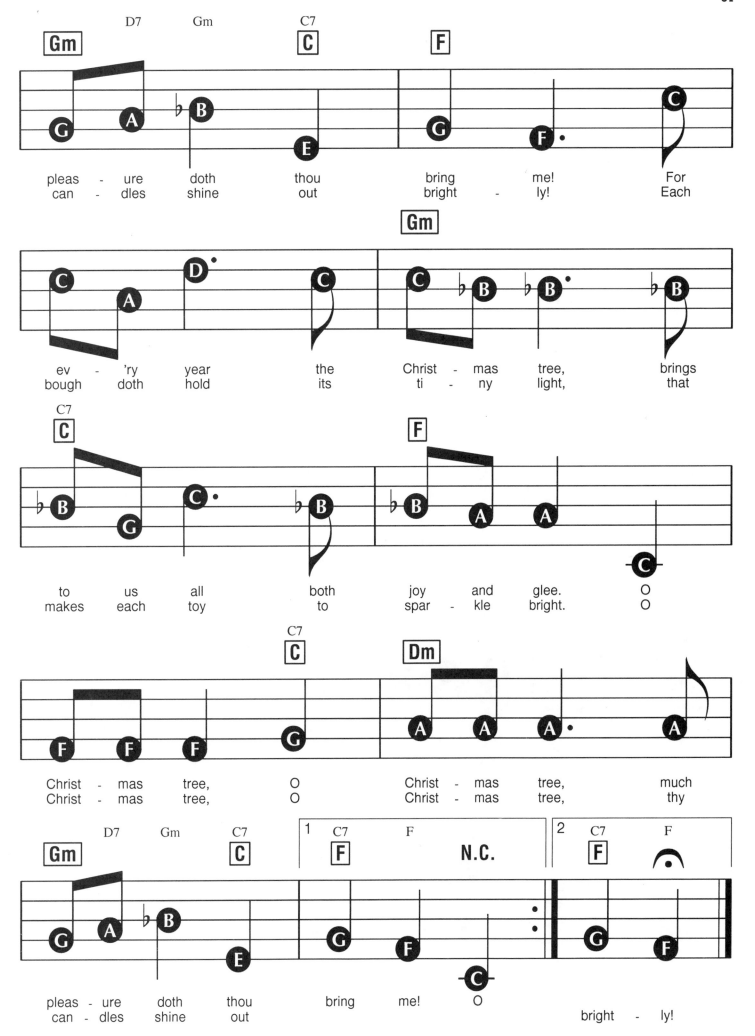

Let It Snow! Let It Snow! Let It Snow!

Registration 2
Rhythm: Fox Trot or Swing

Words by Sammy Cahn
Music by Jule Styne

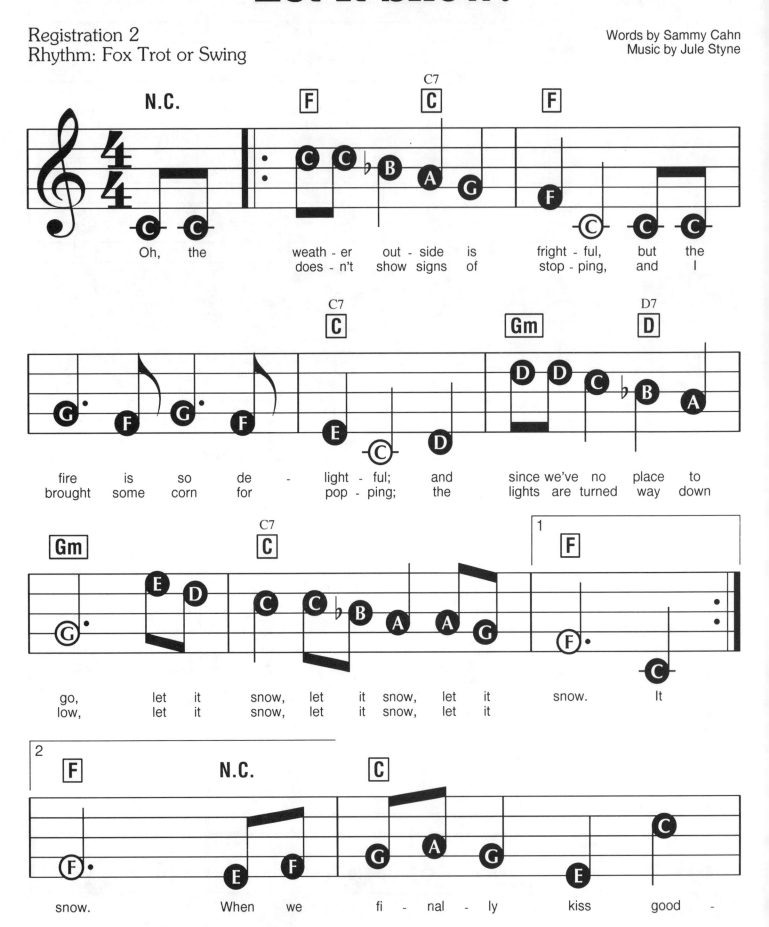

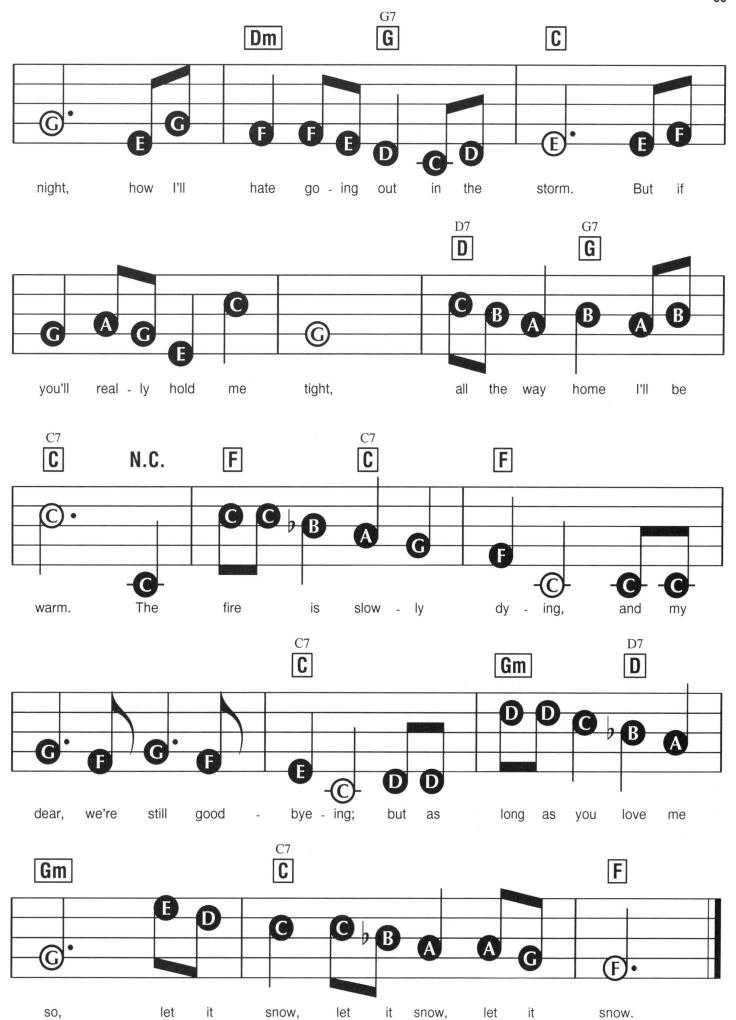

Rockin' Around The Christmas Tree

Registration 2
Rhythm: Swing

Words and Music by
Johnny Marks

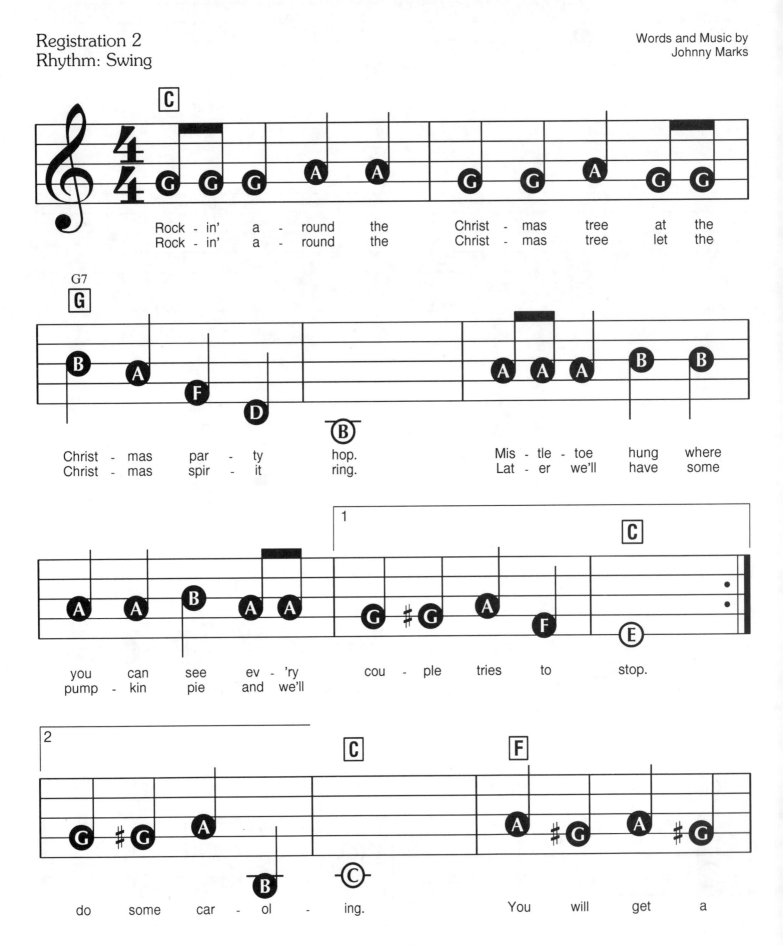

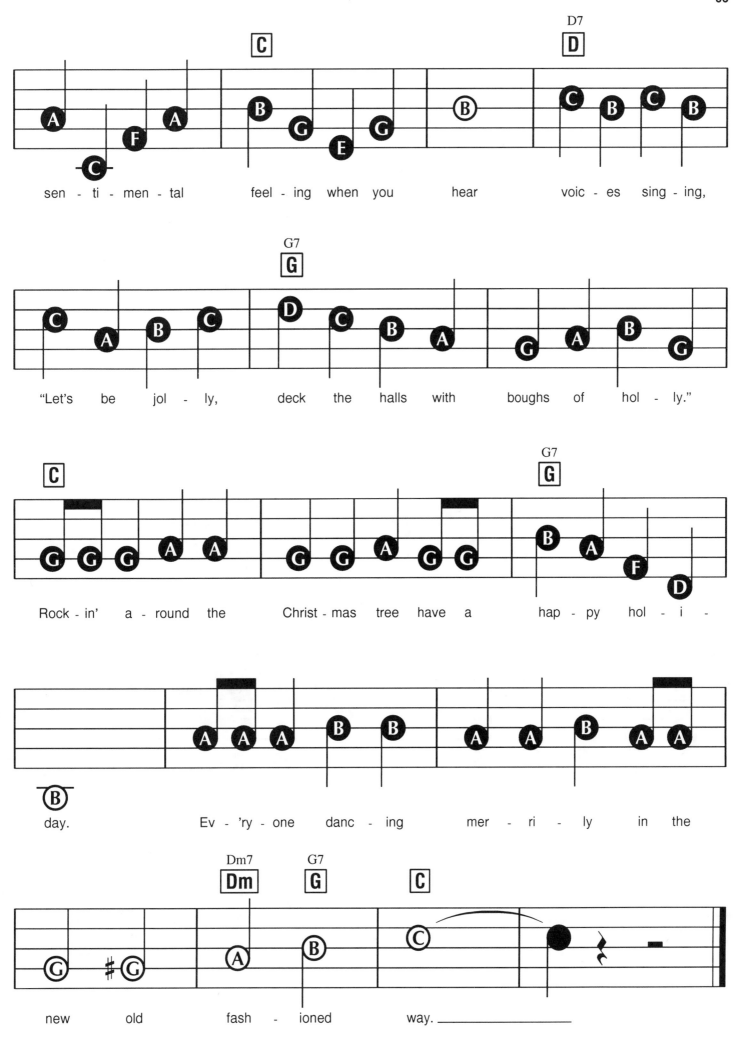

Rudolph The Red-Nosed Reindeer

Registration 4
Rhythm: Fox Trot or Swing

Music and Lyrics by
Johnny Marks

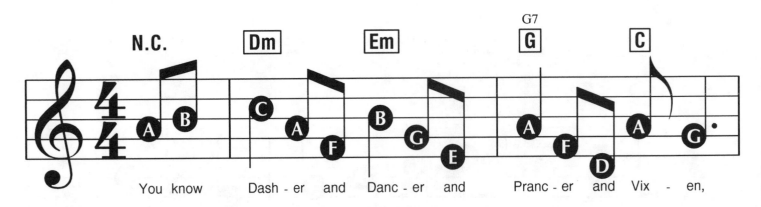

You know Dash - er and Danc - er and Pranc - er and Vix - en,

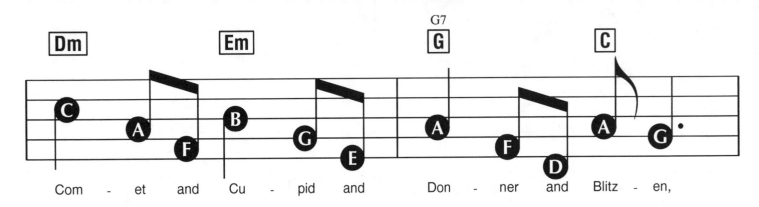

Com - et and Cu - pid and Don - ner and Blitz - en,

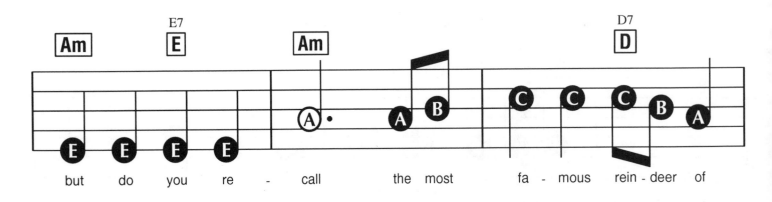

but do you re - call the most fa - mous rein - deer of

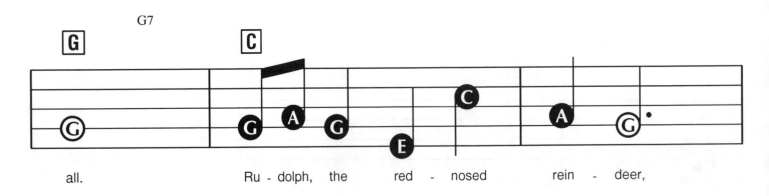

all. Ru - dolph, the red - nosed rein - deer,

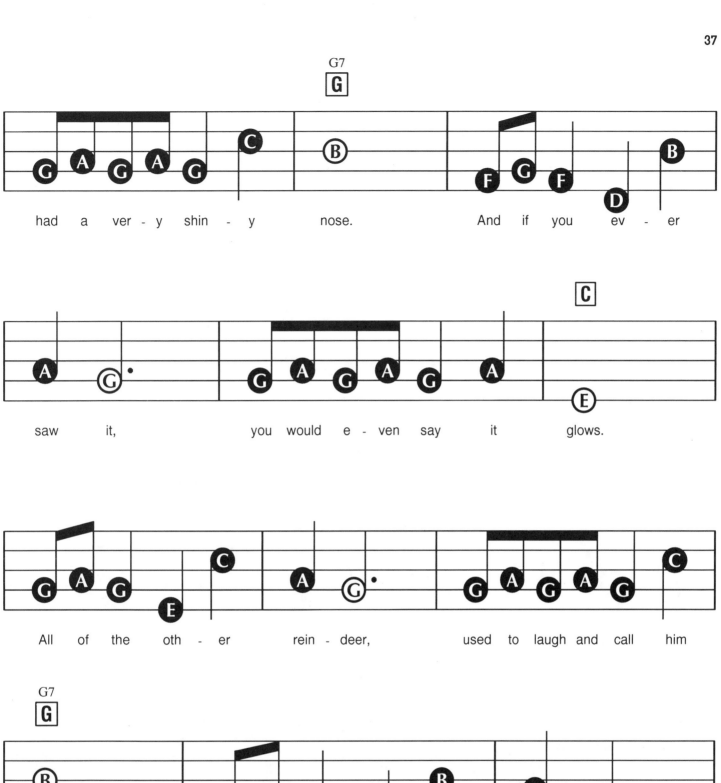

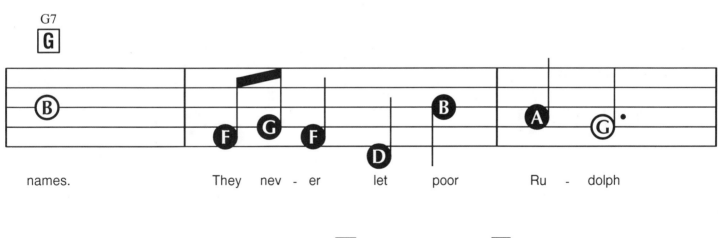

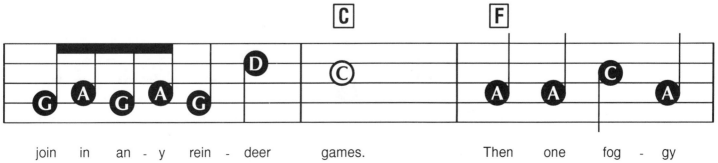

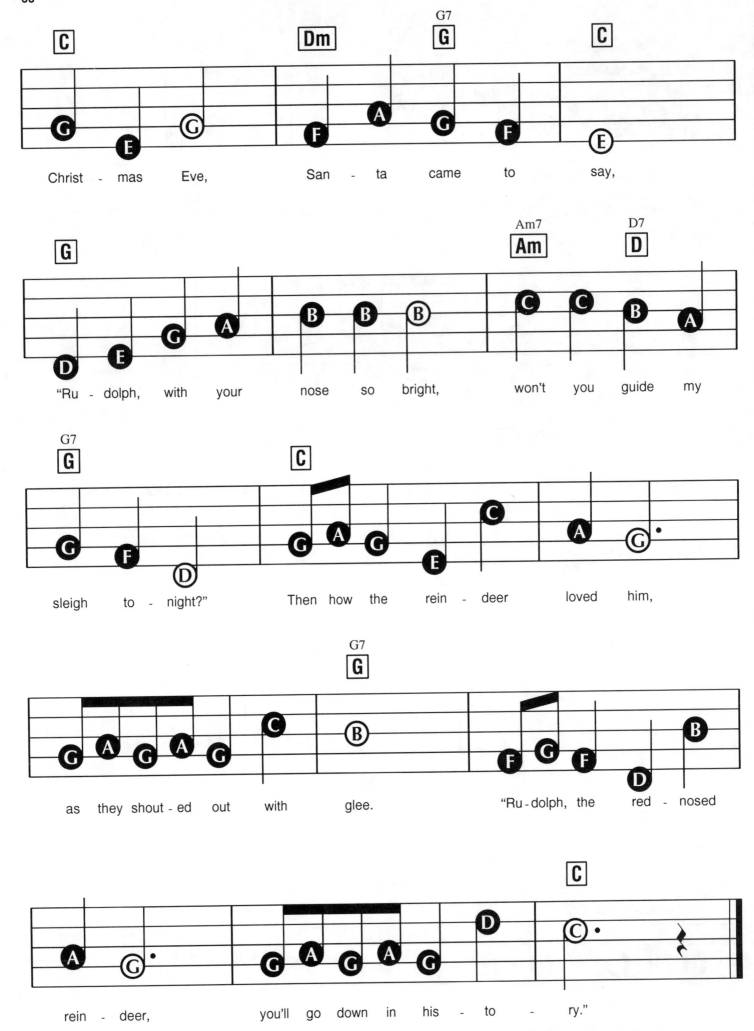

Silver Bells

Registration 7
Rhythm: Waltz

Words and Music by Jay Livingston
and Ray Evans

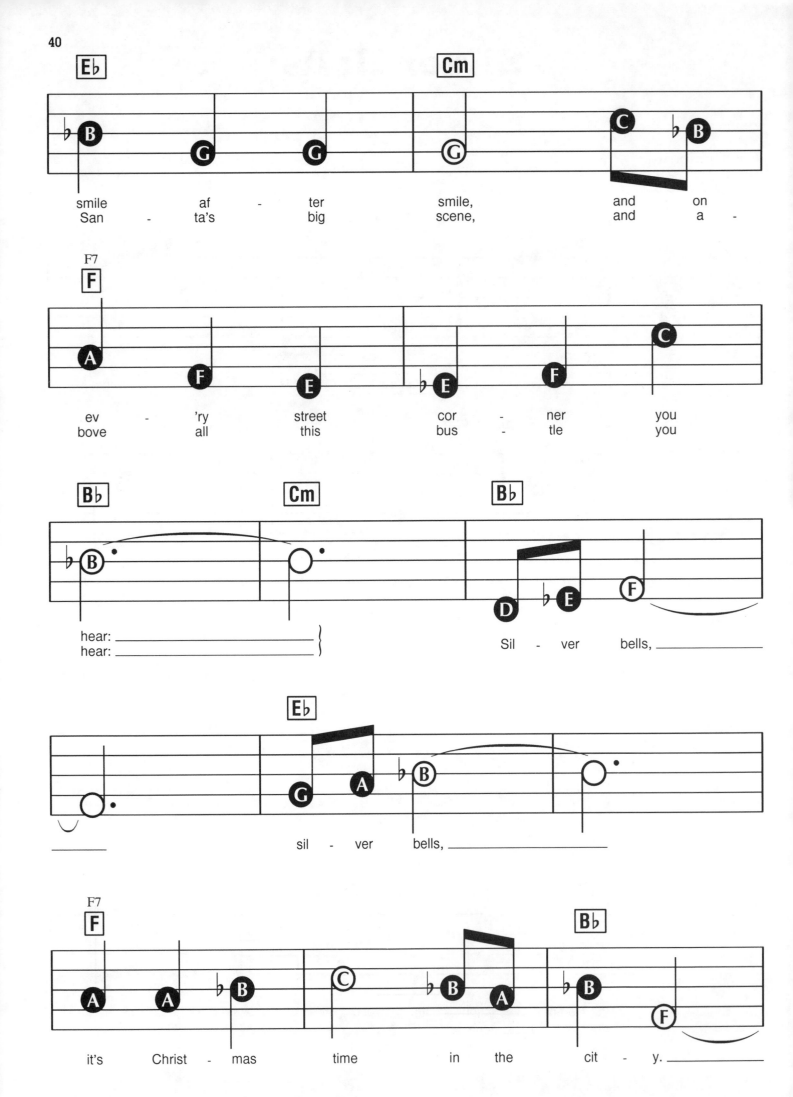

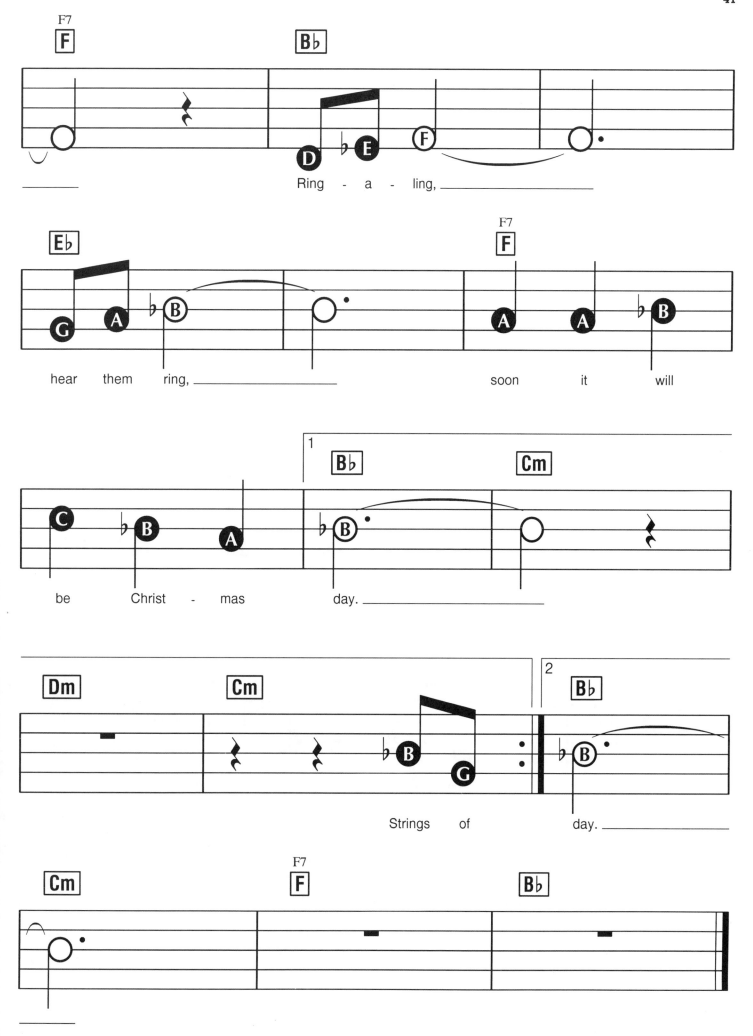

Santa Claus Is Comin' To Town

Registration 4
Rhythm: Swing

Words by Haven Gillespie
Music by J. Fred Coots

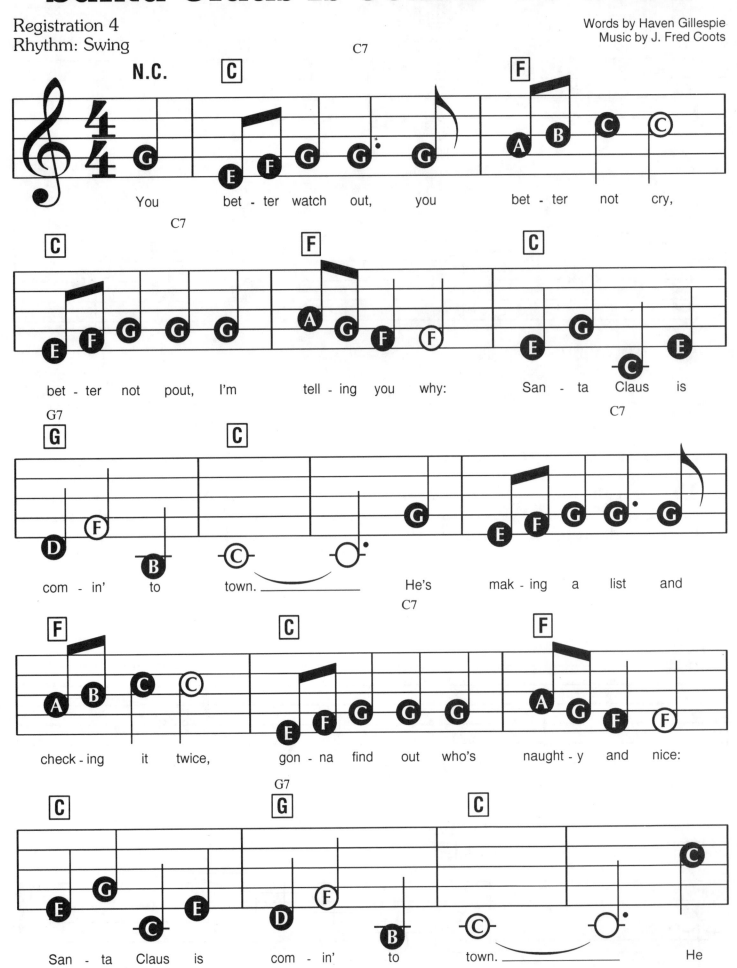

43

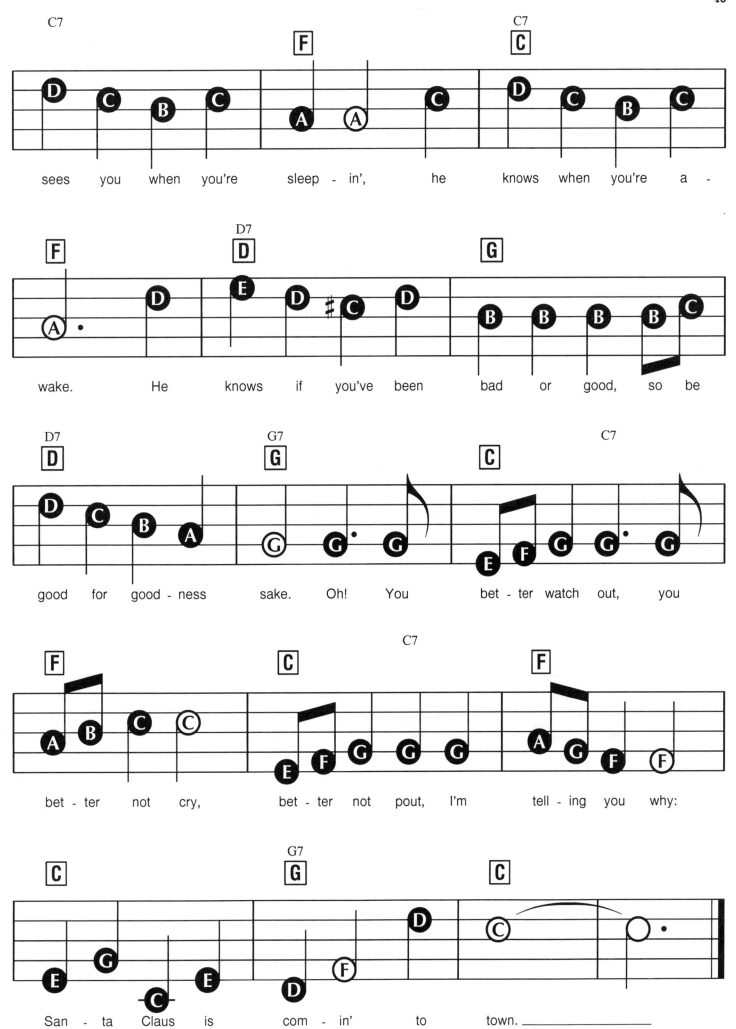

We Wish You A Merry Christmas

Registration 4

Traditional

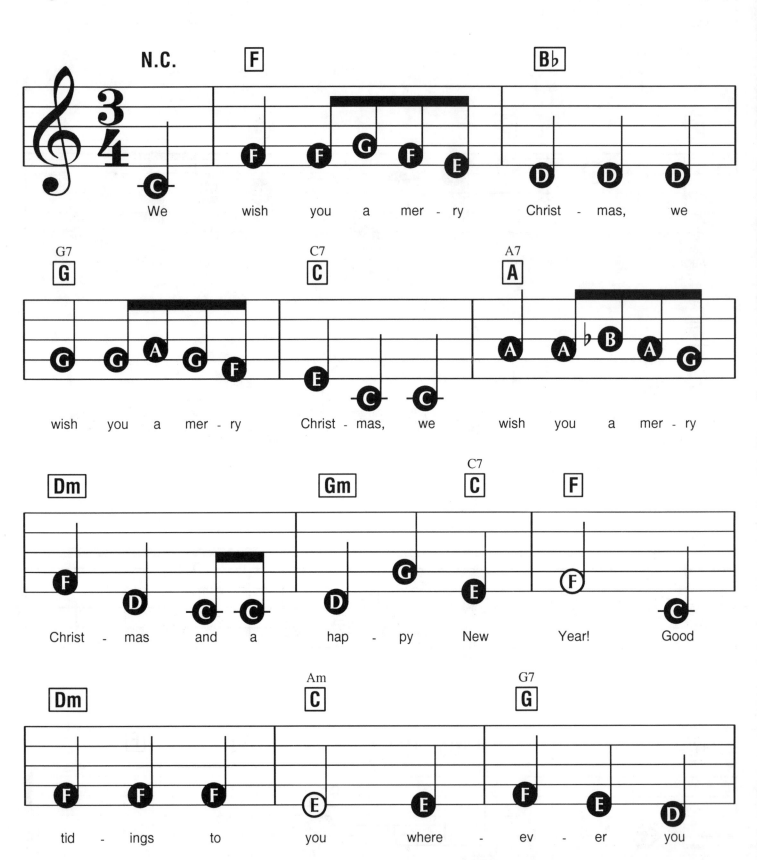

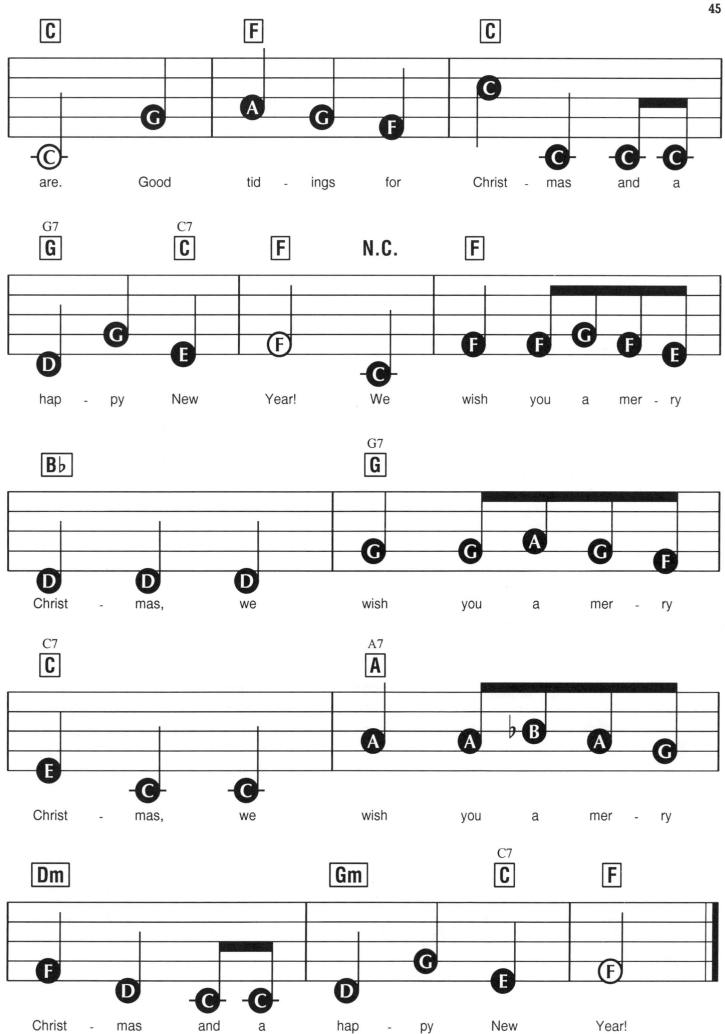

Up On The Housetop

Registration 5
Rhythm: Fox Trot or Swing

Traditional

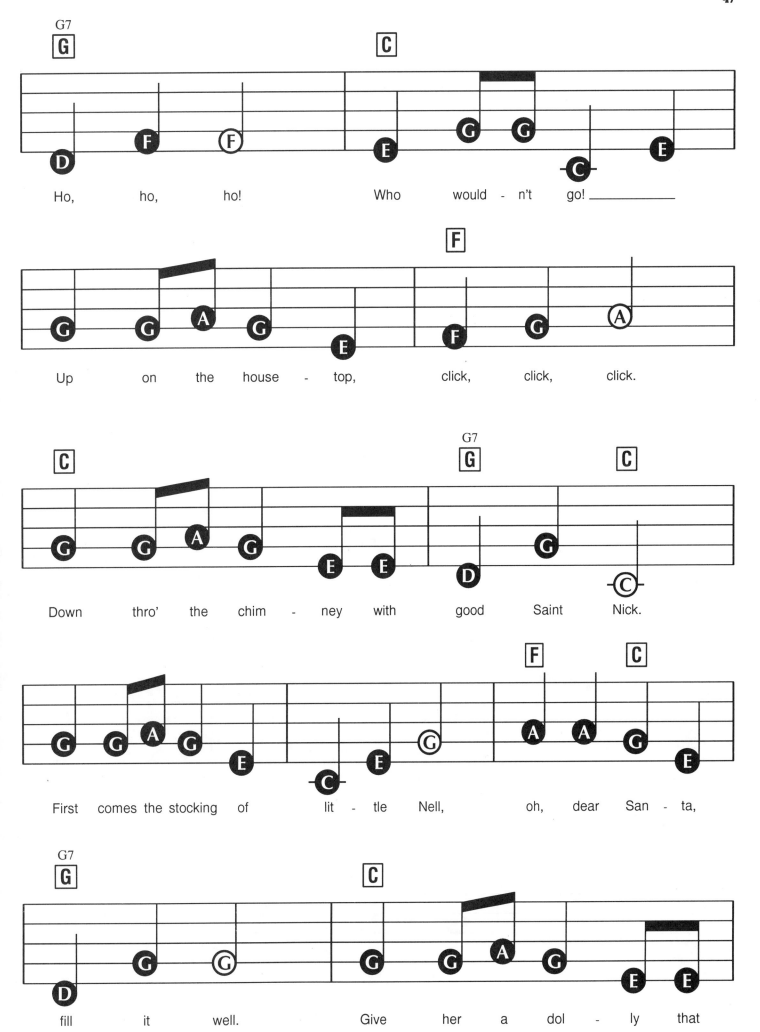

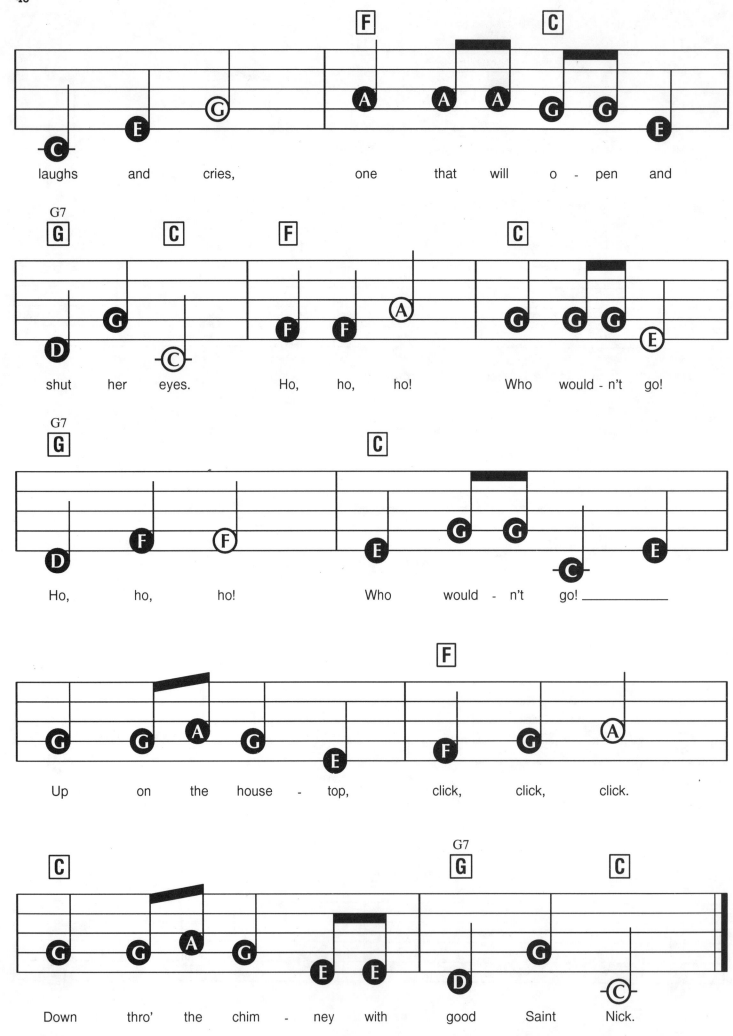